Praise for *Culture Sh*

"With wisdom, love, and a weal[ ]ow nonviolence can be a force for gc[ ]...x and our lives. This book is a treasure. I loc[ ] ...o exploring its many facets with our Zen community."

Roshi Amala Wrightson, director of the Auckland Zen Centre, New Zealand

"*Culture Shift: Nonviolence at Work* is a book to sit with, savor, and most of all: put to work in your life. Kit Miller has distilled a lifetime of experience into a succinct and highly useful collection of field notes for all of us to explore. The ideas are transformative inside and out. The best way to repay this great gift is to use it!"

Rivera Sun, author of *The Dandelion Insurrection* and the Ari Ara Series

"More and more people are aware that the way workplaces function, especially in the US, isn't conducive to human well-being. Far fewer people believe that anything can be done about it and simply adapt as best they can. This book offers a startlingly simple roadmap for creating workplaces where people can breathe, be themselves, and give from their hearts to things that matter to them. Before reading this book, I would have thought it impossible to make the deep essence of nonviolence accessible and so relevant to this task. Kit Miller did just that. Every principle and insight in this book is illustrated with potent stories and anecdotes. Each section ends with reflection questions that support integration and self-trust. And the first few chapters make it deeply clear that there is no jumping over the inside job if we want to change how we function and especially lead in the workplace."

Miki Kashtan, PhD, cofounder of Nonviolent Global Liberation Community, author of *The Highest Common Denominator: Using Convergent Facilitation to Reach Breakthrough Collaborative Decisions*

"Connecting deeply to global outlooks and trends, *Culture Shift: Nonviolence at Work* addresses the urgent need for compassionate and equitable practices in an increasingly interconnected world. Miller's profound insights, shaped by her extensive work with local and international organizations, offer valuable perspectives for navigating the complexities of modern workplaces.

From corporate boardrooms to volunteer organizations, *Culture Shift: Nonviolence at Work* is essential reading for anyone seeking to create meaningful change and foster a more compassionate, equitable, and resilient workplace."

Kobi Skolnick

"I have been working in higher education as a supervisor of people since I began my career. Like most folks, I am reflective of my path. I was brought up to believe that conflict in my professional life was bad, something that should be actively avoided, so I did just that—even when it continued to cost me.

As I pored over the pages in Kit's book, I could not help but reflect on how different my professional life would have been if someone had given me this book. Kit offers readers lessons, 'field notes' where she shares generously what she has learned in her experience. She thoughtfully leads readers through the little-known field of non-violence at work, carefully including every tool that you will need along your journey in this book. Each chapter is bursting with Kit's practical magic, complete with reflection questions for the reader. These were my favorite parts, because it felt like we were in conversation—we, my fellow readers, also have to do some work too.

If you have thought to yourself while at your job, 'I think that things can be different,' this book is for you. If you have wanted to be in a space at your job where no one runs from conflict, but rather learns and grows from it—this book is for you."

Nikkie Herman, director of education, Office of Equity and Inclusion, University of Rochester

"We all need thoughtful invitations and reminders to the essence of the good work we each do every day. In *Culture Shift*, that is exactly what Kit Miller has done for us. Wielding her deep experience and blessing us with so many insights from a rich diversity of activists and thinkers, she offers a path to understanding and practicing nonviolence at our most common site of community: our workplace. As a leader who has struggled with the applicability of nonviolence when facing structural oppression and violence, I found a refreshing and serious approach to facing social justice and community building in principled ways. This is an essential contribution to all our work of improving healthy organizational culture."

Malik Muhammed, EDD, founder of Akoben LLC, author of *The Restorative Journey*

"Conflict today is no longer confined to frontiers and in the public domain. It has entered our personal spaces, in society, in our workplaces, in our homes, and even in our relationships. The most worrying fallout of conflict is how it has anesthetized us to hate and to its consequences, the suffering and misery of those we shrug off as 'others,' and the devastating effect of internecine violence on our environment today, threatening our very existence. We stand at a crossroads, having to choose between extinction and nonviolence—there is no other alternative.

Kit Miller has masterfully written this book about the importance of nonviolence in every sphere of life and how an individual can utilize it in the personal as well as public domain. It is a text book on the ideology of nonviolence and a manual for its practice in the present day.

Life cannot be sustained if we discard nonviolence. This book demystifies nonviolence and teaches the reader how to use it in various circumstances and in various environments."

Tushar A. Gandhi

"Kit Miller's writing exudes a profound humility and simplicity, building on years of hard work, rich experiences, and deep consciousness rooted in nonviolence. Working at personal, interpersonal, and systemic levels, her book offers accessible and impactful practices that anyone can use to bring more peace, cooperation, and aliveness to their workplaces and lives.

Reading this book filled me with belief in a peaceful alternative future for our world, one that any one of us can help create through the 'small' everyday practices and choices that she guides us through."

Kıvanç Çubukçu

"Kit Miller's leadership and capacity to inspire people and groups to collaborate effectively to enact needed social change has long been an inspiration to me. Her book, *Culture Shift: Nonviolence at Work,* is a profound guide to the effective non-violent leadership she embodies. Packed with practical advice, wisdom, and optimism that is grounded in numerous examples from her life and her work, this text helps readers see themselves as leaders and guides them on how to lead with empathy, foster systemic change, and nurture inclusive communities. Miller talks about the importance of finding our heroes—*Culture Shift: Nonviolence at Work* is a keen example of why she is one of mine."

Roxy Manning, PhD

"We may not all be blessed to learn the craft of nonviolence at work in Kit Miller's company, but each of us can sit with the wisdom in this book, knowing every word in it comes from her lived practice."

Dominic Barter

"Imagine yourself in Kit Miller's sunlit kitchen, where over several cups of good coffee she generously shares her abundant recipes for transforming a workplace, organization, neighborhood, or community. Throughout the conversation, she invites you to share and reflect on your own embodied experience. Using the practical and accessible tools of nonviolence, she weaves wisdom from both known and unknown heroes. Kit provides all you need to nourish your own brand of humble, skilled, dynamic, and inclusive leadership—the kind of leadership her life and work exemplify. I celebrate this book which demonstrates how heroic acts of everyday life can and do transform the world."

Anne Symens-Bucher

CULTURE SHIFT
NONVIOLENCE AT WORK

by Kit Miller

Pace e Bene Press

Corvallis, OR

Pace e Bene Press
PO Box F
Corvallis, OR 97339

www.paceebene.org

Culture Shift: Nonviolence at Work by Kit Miller
ISBN-13: 978-0-9978337-3-7
Library of Congress Control Number: 2024942407

Cover design, illustrations, and graphics: Bianca Pointner
Editing and interior layout: Erin Bechtol

We are grateful for permission to use copyrighted material from the following:

Academy for Systems Change, adaptation of "Leverage Points and the Iceberg Model in Economic Development."

Graphic from *Healing Resistance* in Chapter Six "On Conflict," page 80, © with permission of Parallax Press, Berkeley, California, www.parallax.org.

Institute for Health Metrics and Evaluation, adaptation of "Rates of firearm homicides among high-income countries with populations over 10 million, 2021."

Lisa Schirch, adaptation of self, community, and national destruction table.

*Regardless of how and where you spend time
making contributions and bringing in your daily bread,
these notes are for you.*

*Each of you can create spaces with creativity, purpose, and belonging,
offer healing for words and wounds that separate,
break chains, cycles, and barriers.
May these pages nourish your vision, love, and courage.*

Contents

Preface

This book started out as field notes to myself. Field notes are written observations commonly associated with scratch notes, diaries, and journals. They are one way of collecting data that can be combined with interviews and focus groups or stand on their own. What emerged from these notes and interviews with colleagues is a collection of strategies for applying the principles of nonviolence at work.

Why write about work? For one thing "working" hours often comprise more than half of our waking lives, whether paid or unpaid. For the purpose of this book, I include volunteer activities, activism, study, engagement with faith communities, our neighborhoods, and other groups as part of our work. Figuring out how to incorporate nonviolence into the daily grind can make your one precious life as nourishing, wholehearted, and influential as possible.

Research on mental health and trauma indicates that many, even most, people alive today are living lives of relational poverty, deprived of meaningful connection with others.[1] The impacts of our disconnections are sobering: anxiety, addiction, suicide, and more. It makes good sense to start meeting needs for community, meaning, learning, and dignity in mentally-healthy groups and work. The interviews for this book shared a heartening theme: by including nonviolence in our approach to work, we can head home even after full, challenging days, able to bring life-giving skills to our relationships.

The approaches described here create the potential for what socioogist Asef Bayat calls "social non-movements": the collective actions of individuals

---

1. Bruce Perry and Oprah Winfrey, *What Happened to You?: Conversations on Trauma, Resilience, and Healing*, "Chapter 9: Relational Hunger in the Modern World."

whose activities trigger social change.[2] Further, many of the practices—from relaxing with complexity to leveraging what already works—are also research-based means to address polarization, described by Peter Coleman in *The Way Out: How to Overcome Toxic Polarization*.

There is tremendous potential for using our lives as a lever for change, with cascading benefits for ourselves, colleagues, students, clients, family, friends, and communities. Isn't that great?

Since words can be such blunt instruments, some definitions are included. Opportunities to pause and reflect are sprinkled throughout. A few project stories illustrate some of the principles described. I hope that a team or group you participate in might pick out some sections to read and reflect on.

We are never without help.
Look for it always
to surprise you.
—Alice Walker

As you read, I hope you feel my gratitude for the thousands of people who gave rise to these ideas. I draw inspiration from countless people I have learned from, precious friends, family, colleagues, and a handful of teachers and elders who have shaped the content of this book.

Through this work, you are connected with Arun Gandhi, friend, author, and cofounder with his wife Sunanda of the M. K. Gandhi Institute for Nonviolence. Through conversations, projects, and learning-packed trips to India and to South Africa with the Gandhi Legacy Tour, studying the lives of Gandhi and of Nelson Mandela, I have felt how a lifelong connection to nonviolence can become embodied in human beings. With Arun, I had the honor of time with some of my heroes: Archbishop Desmond Tutu, who instigated the Truth and Reconciliation Commission in South Africa, and his daughter Mpho in Cape Town, South Africa; and Vandana Shiva, scientist, author, activist, and ecofeminist, at her farm outside Dehradun, India.

Arun was interviewed for these field notes, and was enthusiastic about writing a foreword. He was an esteemed, supportive thought partner on many of the efforts described. Along with thousands of others, I am grieved by his passing on May 2, 2023. Rest in power, dear peace farmer! We miss you.

---

2. Doris H. Grey and Nadia Sonneveld, *Women and Social Change in North Africa: What Counts as Revolutionary?*, 5.

You are connected to Dr. Bernard Lafayette Jr., who asked for a "write up" of the approach my colleagues and I were using to practice nonviolence at work. "Doc," as he is called by many, was a young Black college student when he became engaged in the civil rights movement, working directly with Dr. King. He has spent six decades developing curricula and teaching Kingian Nonviolence to tens of thousands of people. His request evolved into this book.

You are connected with Marshall Rosenberg, the creator of the Nonviolent Communication process. I was privileged to work with Marshall in a number of capacities—as a Center for Nonviolent Communication board member 1999-2004, as a coordinator for numerous events, and as a person who supported him in a variety of ways.

You are connected with Joanna Macy, antinuclear and enviromental activist, author, and scholar of Buddhism, systems theory, and ecology. Joanna has been a gift in my life via time spent in her retreats, one-on-one, and in other settings courtesy of my friend Anne Symens-Bucher. This book could be filled with appreciation for Joanna and her bold, brilliant teaching, including this framework of three co-existent stories playing out for humanity that shapes my perspectives on nonviolence at work:

- Business as usual: current systems that generate inequality, polarity, violence, and devastation on a planetary scale.
- The Great Unraveling: the consequences of business as usual, with accelerating rates of harm within, between, and among people and to life itself.
- The Great Turning: the thousands of movements, projects, and organizations that seek to address harm, as well as experiments with new forms of thought and action within every field.[3]

This book represents efforts and experiments in nonviolence as part of the Great Turning. I feel grateful to be part of this significant shift in human history—and for good company along the way. Much of the content was cocreated in the inspiring company of colleagues at Bay Area Nonviolent Communication in Oakland, California, where I served as director from 2004 to 2009, and then at the M. K. Gandhi Institute in Rochester, New York, where I again served as director from 2009 to 2021. They contributed years of experience in practicing nonviolence at work, which they gifted me while writing this book. I interviewed eighteen Gandhi Institute staff and board members, past and present, to check and double check my assumptions. Thank you all! Additionally, this content has been field-tested

---

3. Joanna Macy, *World as Lover, World as Self.*

in numerous retreats and countless workshops with many people whose feedback guided the choices of what to include here. If we have hung out together in one of those spaces, thank you for helping me to trust these ideas.

Rivera Sun contributed many hours of support via editing and conversations. Bianca Pointner created the images and art with such love. Erin Bechtol offered gifts of time, precision, and enthusiasm in the months we spent editing together.

I feel enormously grateful for financial support and for precise feedback on drafts from my beautiful friend Rick Smith. Maja Bengston offered valuable insight during the editing, overcoming challenges with reading in her third language! Maisha Enaharo, Anne Symens-Bucher, Dominic Barter, Miki Kashtan, and Rashid Muhammed contributed via countless hours of friendship, support, and collaborations. Sometimes it is hard to know when and where ideas and approaches were generated. Forgive me, friends, when I have overlooked attributions.

I feel gratitude to indigenous cultures everywhere for their example and generous teachings, especially to the Haudenosaunee people on whose unceded lands my family has lived for 140 years.

I live in gratitude for the waters and hills of the Finger Lakes, for Lake Ontario, and for the oaks, maples, and other trees. I remember breathing in this moment is your gift.

I feel grateful for the profound teachings of parenthood, and for our son, Alec, our daughter-in-law, Carrie, and for our daughters, Molly and Audrey. Last and far from least, my remarkable husband, David, has offered loving, enthusiastic support for more than thirty years. We have walked through fires together with love. The differences between us teach me how rich and rewarding it is to be in relation to those who challenge our thinking.

Invoking this web lifts my heart, and I hope yours too. It offers a chance to see this book as emerging from thousands of people's love and attention. May this bring you a sense of solidarity, friendship, and connection across time and space.

—Kit Miller

Chapter One
Leadership and Nonviolence at Work

Everyone is a leader. Maybe you already know that you are one, or you hope to be one, or you sense leadership being thrust upon you. You may be a leader in a small group, in your family, or at a nonprofit or large institution. You may be a leader because of your job or position. You may be a leader because you dance to your own tune and inspire others.

I am a leader too. This is partly because of position and circumstance, and partly because I am not afraid to take risks, try things, and leap into the fray. I have served as the director of two organizations. I've facilitated hundreds of workshops, dialogues and meetings, and many retreats. I've cofounded numerous projects. I've initiated and joined campaigns for social justice. I am a leader within my extended family. Each role teaches another set of lessons.

These notes describe skills, practices, and understandings useful for embodying leadership and for conducting experiments to transform workplaces into responsive living systems. In a living system, leadership feels like gardening—we try to create the best conditions for roses to bloom, cabbages to sprout, and moss to flourish. In a living system we recognize and enact the understanding that means and ends are bound together.

Leadership in a living system is about showing up in all aspects of our lives, especially when we fall short. It's recognizing that in hundreds of ways we have more power than we have been conditioned to see. It's seeking to breathe humanity—and therefore sustainability—as a discipline into policies and practices. In leadership positions, we have the ability to effect change, shift people's views, rewire and construct systems, and more. Finally, leadership is about understanding power, including the power of cultural conditioning, and taking responsibility for it. This is where nonviolence at work comes in.

Nonviolence at Work

Nonviolence supports and compels us to move out of our conditioned acceptance of powerless identities and to take responsibility for change in any way, at any scale. In a culture laced with more forms of violence than we can count, nonviolence invites us to move toward our potential as changemakers in personal, political, and professional ways.

Nonviolence is often misunderstood. Encompassing far more than the absence of violence, the field of nonviolence includes thousands of skills, practices, and actions. Nonviolence has been described in many ways—as a philosophy or way of life, a science or art, a toolbox for change, a set of solutions and alternatives, and so forth. The King Center in Atlanta, Georgia, defines nonviolence as a love-centered way of thinking, speaking, acting, and engaging that leads to personal, cultural, and societal transformation. In short, nonviolence is not passivity, or weakness, or doing nothing.

Nonviolence at work takes a thousand forms. Here are a few you might recognize:

- Standing up for colleagues who are overlooked.
- Helping coworkers (and others) sort out a conflict.

- Changing discriminatory and unjust policies.
- Ensuring events and services are accessible to all.
- Speaking up when there's a problem.
- Taking responsibility for solving problems, regardless of who created them.
- Challenging mistreatment.
- Asking for help rather than going it alone.

If you lead your life this way already, or are trying to, and don't think of it as nonviolence, that's OK. Even without that intentional framing, these approaches are still powerful. In word and action, over time, they do more good and less harm. They contribute to the kind of nonviolence that Dr. Martin Luther King Jr., James Lawson, M. K. Gandhi, Dorothy Day, and others lived, and are also described as principled nonviolence. I invite you to try out this perspective—that you may be acting nonviolently—while reading and see how it feels.

Before we head into these notes, let's first think together about violence. What is it, and what are we seeking to change?

On Violence

If violence was truly natural to humanity then we would not be harmed by participating in or even witnessing it.

—Paul K. Chappell

Every relationship of domination, of exploitation, of oppression is by definition violent, whether or not the violence is expressed by drastic means. In such a relationship, dominator and dominated alike are reduced to things—the former dehumanized by an excess of power, the latter by a lack of it. And things cannot love.

—Paulo Freire

Violence is so normalized that we don't recognize the harm to our emotional, psychological, and spiritual well-being—it is the unhealthy water that we swim in. I was taught to recognize violence primarily as physical harm—fist fights, guns, bombs, war. As many of us are coming to understand, violence takes a multitude of forms, as both root cause and consequence.

Millions of words have been written about violence. For this book, we will use definitions from Johan Galtung, a scholar in the field of peacebuilding:

- **Structural violence** is the systematic way in which some groups are hindered from access to opportunities, goods, and services to enable the fulfillment of basic human needs. These can be formal legal structures (such as Jim Crow laws). They could be culturally functional but without legal mandate (such as limited access to education for marginalized groups).

- **Cultural Violence** describes the existence of prevailing social norms that make direct and structural violence seem "natural" or "right" or at least acceptable.[4] Healthcare outcomes that are reflective of medical providers' bias are one example of cultural violence.

Structural and cultural violence create the conditions for the interpersonal forms of violence that we are taught to recognize as violence. Here are examples at the level of self, community, and nation from researcher Lisa Schirch:[5]

SELF DESTRUCTION	COMMUNITY DESTRUCTION	NATIONAL DESTRUCTION
Alcohol and drug abuse	Crime	Terrorism
Internalized oppression	Interpersonal violence	Rebel groups
Suicide	Domestic violence	Civil wars
Depression	Rape	Coups

There is a common cultural script that *violence is someone's fault*—an individual bad actor or set of actors, like the ones we see in the movies, or corrupt individuals within an organization like a business or government. To address that violence, all we have to do is identify and punish the actors and—presto, problem solved! Most problem solving about violence in the media and through political processes represents this "bad actor/actors" framework. Change the players, and all will be well.

---

4. Johan Galtung, "Cultural Violence," *Journal of Peace Research* 27, no. 3. (August, 1990): 291-305.
5. Lisa Schirch, *The Little Book of Strategic Peacebuilding: A Vision And Framework For Peace With Justice.*

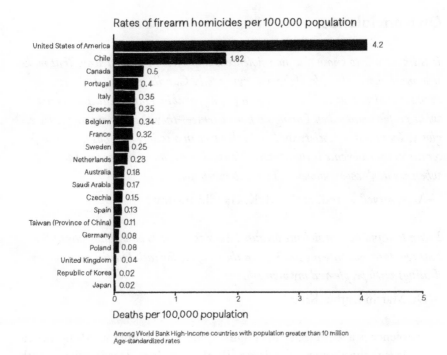

Rates of firearm homicides per 100,000 population

Country	Rate
United States of America	4.2
Chile	1.82
Canada	0.5
Portugal	0.4
Italy	0.35
Greece	0.35
Belgium	0.34
France	0.32
Sweden	0.25
Netherlands	0.23
Australia	0.18
Saudi Arabia	0.17
Czechia	0.15
Spain	0.13
Taiwan (Province of China)	0.11
Germany	0.08
Poland	0.08
United Kingdom	0.04
Republic of Korea	0.02
Japan	0.02

Deaths per 100,000 population

Among World Bank High-Income countries with population greater than 10 million
Age-standardized rates

The problem is that this approach does not work in reality. Research data says the results are in on this. For instance, despite incarcerating more people than any other nation, and spending billions on elections for politicians who vow to solve the issue, the US leads high income nations globally in gun violence.

Other countries now issue warnings to their citizens regarding travel to the US.[7] Our thinking and level of response continues the problem. As Arun Gandhi said, "Violence only destroys fellow human beings, it never solves, or destroys, conflict itself."[8] We can—and must—learn to respond in new ways.

Your turn: What have you been taught about violence? Where do those messages come from? When you think about issues of violence—internal, interpersonal, or systemic—do you feel clarity on how to respond, or something else? Have you visited any of the countries listed in the graphic above? Have you felt different levels of safety based on your location?

6. https://www.healthdata.org/acting-data/gun-violence-united-states-outlier
7. https://www.cnn.com/travel/article/travel-warnings-other-countries-us-violence/index.html
8. https://www.youtube.com/watch?v=rM-H4jb5BU8

On Nonviolence

It is important to know that nonviolence is imperfect in the best way. That makes it so much more relatable. We're not trying to be Gandhi or King. We're trying to make choices that reduce harm as much as possible. Harm reduction is not what people want when I bring up nonviolence—they want something perfect, glossy. That's not the society we live in. We live in a society that has taught us for centuries that violence is the answer. Nonviolence is all of the spaces that exist when we don't choose violence. There's so much space!

—Alex, served as staff at the M. K. Gandhi Institute

I plan to stand by nonviolence because I have found it to be a philosophy of life that regulates not only my dealings in the struggle for racial justice but also my dealings with people and my own self.

—Dr. Martin Luther King Jr.

Nonviolence is a word that can conjure up dozens of other words by association. It isn't the absence of violence. Think about how doctors take an oath to "first, do no harm." This is just the beginning of all the ways in which they can support patients' healing and well-being. Similarly, nonviolence encompasses hundreds of practices, ideas, approaches, and tools. We get the term *nonviolence* from Gandhi. It is an almost direct translation of the Sanskrit, *ahimsa*. In that ancient language, *himsa* means *harm*. The prefix *a-* is the negation of harm. Rather than simply meaning the absence of harm, however, it invokes the presence of all things non-harming. Take a look at this word map of terms connected to nonviolence:

Love   Respect   Healing
                                        Justice
Liberation   Compassion
                              Living Wages
March   Regenerative   Protest
                    Dignity
Action   Health   Nonviolence
                                        Nurturing
          Fair Trade   Self-Care
Fairness   Boycott
          Restorative
Well-Being   Replenishing   Soulforce
              Transformation
    Trauma Healing   Liberation

What words would you add?

As you see, vocabulary related to nonviolence is an art, not a science. Nonviolence is generous—it doesn't care what we call it.

Over time, numerous people have given me the gift of expressing skepticism about nonviolence. It's a gift because their expression opens up the possibility of a conversation. If they are willing, I ask them to think it through with me. Are they objecting to nonviolence as an internal approach, or interpersonally, or on institutional or state levels? The majority of concerns center on interpersonal violence and the need for self-defense. We agree that almost all people want to have a more peaceful inner life, with fewer harsh self-judgments. Almost all of us prefer warm or cordial relationships with colleagues, friends, neighbors, and family. Similarly, most would prefer resolving global disputes through strategies like trade and diplomacy, rather than arms races and war.[9]

As people articulate these shared ideals, I find that the objection to nonviolence as a whole shrinks. What remains is a conversation about the need for physical safety. In that sphere, there is much to learn, from conflict de-escalation strategies to martial arts (like aikido where the focus is on defense, not aggression).

Like Quaker activist and nonviolence advocate George Lakey, I believe that "nonviolence is not a method to prevent conflict. It is a method to conduct conflict." Conflict offers transformative, necessary energy for change. Nonviolence offers methods of harnessing that energy and is available to all people.

Consider this: if we can have violence in all layers of society, we can also have *nonviolence* in all layers of society. Instead of staying stuck in cycles of violence, we can break this pattern with healing, transformative, and liberatory practices. Imagine if:

- every employer paid fair wages to workers;
- organizations replaced discriminatory policies with equitable ones;
- factories took wholehearted responsibility for every byproduct of the manufacturing processes;

9. "The success of nonviolent civil resistance: Erica Chenoweth at TEDxBoulder," https://www.youtube.com/watch?v=YJSehRlU34w.

- each industry repaired and restored the earth and the people it inter-
  acted with; and
- all jobs came with safety, pensions, and dignity.

The byproducts—or secondary nonviolence—of such examples of structural nonviolence could include better mental and physical health, improved family relations including reduced domestic violence, racial healing, increased civic activism, healthier ecosystems, time for creative and spiritual pursuits—the list is long, and lovely. We can experience what I think of as collateral healing. Isn't that a vision worth thinking about, practicing, and working toward?

Your turn: What have you been taught about nonviolence? Where do those messages come from? What do you wonder now about nonviolence?

Picture Nonviolence at Work

The immediate need of our time is for ripened and seasoned adult human beings to take their place in our communities; individuals who carry a deep and abiding fidelity to the living body of this benevolent earth, to beauty, and to their own souls.
—Francis Weller

Recently resettled families from Afghanistan are now living around the Institute. They have a key to the house and are using it for gatherings. I came to the house one day and they were cooking, the space smelled amazing, all the aunties and grandmothers together. It's a safe space and a creative space. It felt really good to see them use the space.
—Bianca, served as staff at the M. K. Gandhi Institute

The red house sits on the crest of a slight rise, a vegetable garden tumbling down the hillside next to it. From my office on the second floor, I could see the bustle of the street, the buses lumbering past, and people walking down the sidewalks. In the next room, my colleagues' voices rumbled and lilted. The scent of lentils and rice rose up from the kitchen downstairs. That evening in the warm, yellow common room, friends of the M. K. Gandhi Institute would be gathering to share stories and connect around our care for our community. As I turned to my computer to dig into my inbox, I could hear footsteps in the hall and the hush that infused the workplace chatter when someone used the meditation room.

This is nonviolence at work. So were our debates during staff meetings, and uncomfortable confrontations with injustice in various settings, and the cacophony of training two dozen young humans in conflict resolution skills. It offers a glimpse of a different way to be. Picture it: You get up and go to work—perhaps repairing houses or driving a bus or teaching children or healing people. Whatever "work" looks like, throughout your day you feel safe, nourished, and connected. Your skills and talents construct projects or services that help people, communities, and the earth. At the end of the day, you know you've contributed something positive. At home, there's a spring in your step. You have energy for family, roommates, partners, friends, studies, and community work.

Too few of us experience this. Our society churns out violence as its default setting. As noted earlier, it's not only physical—violence is also systemic, structural, cultural, emotional, and more. In the workplace, this violence takes forms including overwork, wage theft, sexual harassment, exploitation, exposure to hazardous materials, unsafe practices, racism, and sexism. Can we enact another way? I know we can.

The M. K. Gandhi Institute was founded in 1991 by Arun and Sunanda Gandhi. Arun was a grandson of Mohandas K. Gandhi, and offered a steady, supportive presence for the organization. He was a frequent participant in our community dinners and was very engaged with the work we did in prisons in our area. Sunanda Gandhi was a nurse and dedicated, compassionate activist who passed away in 2007. When I first started in my role as the director of the Institute, our mission was to "educate, embody, and serve" through nonviolence. We teach nonviolence, conflict skills, restorative justice, and offer innovative programs to support youth. We join and support movements for change. We assist individuals and institutions in recognizing and finding ways to dismantle structural violence and systemic injustice. And—*what* we do isn't as important as *how* we do it.

An organization like the Gandhi Institute can embody nonviolence in its choices, policies, relationship to community, etc., including: How to choose projects? Relate to other groups? Treat its people? Make decisions? Engage its supporters, both donors and volunteers?

Answering these questions offers hundreds of chances to practice nonviolence. Every choice that you and your organizations make can either comply with the norms of a violent culture, or pull a different future into being.

Transforming places where we spend time, paid or unpaid, is a tall order. However, as Buddhist teacher and peace activist Thich Nhat Hanh said, "Nonviolence is a direction, not a separating line." Instead of doing nothing because *everything* is overwhelming, let's do *some things* and keep nudging the world in the direction of nonviolence. During my years at the M. K. Gandhi Institute, my colleagues and I made dozens of small shifts. I've discovered that these nudges were not insignificant. For the people they impact, they are profoundly meaningful, restoring a sense of dignity, wholeness, and trust to the place where they give so much of their precious lives. From work with dozens of organizations—healthcare, government, banks, faith communities, and schools—I have witnessed that positive changes are possible in any setting.[10]

Your Turn: What would change in your field, industry, or work if everyone tried to "first, do no harm" and then tried to embody nonviolence? Do some dreaming about the possibilities, write it down, and save it as a record of your vision and commitment. It's OK not to know how it will happen— dream anyway.

Chapter One Key Ideas

- Everyone is a leader. Nonviolent leadership allows us to emphasize humanity in our policies and practices.
- Nonviolence at work is active and collaborative.
- Violence—including structural and cultural violence—is normalized and pervasive at every level of society.
- Nonviolence offers "a method to conduct conflict."
- Nonviolence at work can guide individuals, groups, and organizations toward prioritizing dignity, trust, and wholeness consistently.

---

10. Current research on building trauma-informed organizations supports the approaches described in this chapter. To see some of that research and for more information on trauma-informed organizations, see https://www.dralishamorelandcapuia.com/.

Chapter Two
The Inside Job

We build the road and the road builds us.

—Sarvodaya Movement, Sri Lanka

Thirty years ago, I changed jobs. I shifted from being a well-paid sales-person to being an unpaid, stay-at-home mom. At the time, I thought the big leap we were making was financial—and for me, that was a big leap, indeed. My family history of alcoholism and the resulting stress had oriented me toward a focus on safety via financial security.

This career change was prompted by an epiphany of sorts. In the early 1990s, I volunteered at a small urban hospice center called Isaiah House.

We offered care for people of diverse socioeconomic backgrounds, mostly dying from cancer or AIDS. Those weekly four-hour shifts changed the trajectory of my life for many reasons, but the most significant one was realizing what mattered most to people at the end of their lives. Regardless of race, age, gender, occupation, income and wealth, education, or any other factor, the individuals I met at Isaiah House seemed to focus on how well they connected with their close relations—or didn't. Even as I write this sentence, I can see the faces of the many people who felt this way. After observing this over and over again, I felt clear that I would regret continuing to be a working mom after our youngest child was born. I did not want to look back at my life and lament the missed time with my children. Fortunately for my family, it was possible, though it required sacrifice, for me to stay home.

Fr. Richard Rohr says, "We put off enlightenment by decades if we are not present for births and deaths."[11] I did not experience enlightenment by having children, or by caring for the dying. I did become less ignorant about what most mattered to me. It broke the substantial hold that financial security had exercised over my priorities, including my education and career to date.

So, I quit—and it was quietly disastrous.

It turned out that the real big leap I was making (we were making) wasn't financial, but something else entirely. For the same reasons that I had succeeded in the business world, I was deeply unsuited for this new job of full-time mother. From the time I was very young, my parents, schooling, and culture, had all trained me to focus on outcomes and goals. I had little capacity for presence and patience—two of the qualities that children thrive on. Within weeks, it became clear that being a goals-driven mom was generating pain and distress for me and for all of us.

I had already started a meditation practice. Meditation holds up a mirror— and sometimes the image feels unbearable. I began to notice the lightning speed of frequent, venomous self-judgments. When I believed and reacted from these thoughts, they produced harshness and impatience, and spilled out onto others. So much grief, past and present, surfaced. Additionally, as a child I experienced some physical violence; I saw the potential in myself to fall into those behaviors too. I began to wonder if it would be better for

---

11. Richard Rohr, *Immortal Diamond: The Search for Our True Self,* 141.

everyone if I went back to work and hired someone kinder and gentler to care for our children.[12]

The realization about the importance of relationships from hospice work stopped me from seeing this as a possibility. My beautiful husband, David, believed in me when I doubted myself. So instead of going back to work, I dedicated myself to transforming rather than transferring the violence I experienced. I began by studying various forms of nonviolence, starting with mindfulness and Nonviolent Communication. It was a steep and sometimes painful climb that has become a life-sustaining path.

The study of nonviolence led me to pursue sustainability and education reform as vehicles for transformation, along with deep ecology, systems thinking, anti-racism work, restorative justice, and permaculture. Reading Gandhi and learning about Kingian Nonviolence principles from people like Dr. Bernard Lafayette and Dr. James Lawson helped to reveal connections between these apparently disparate disciplines.

"We build the road and the road builds us." This is the motto of the Sri Lankan Sarvodaya Movement, a decades-long nonviolent movement to achieve well-being and dignity for everyone, all together. The work we do—with muscles, minds, hearts, skills, talents, and resources—not only builds something in the community, it builds something within us. The converse is also true, of course. The work we do inside deeply shapes the work we are able to do for our organizations and world. For me, the inside job precedes outer occupation. In this chapter, we'll dig into ways of enacting nonviolence within.

Your Turn: When have you made a leap into the unknown? As you reflect on it now, what did you learn from that leap? Who in your life supports you to think about making courageous moves?

Words: Windows or Walls

Sound is dynamic. Speech is dynamic—it is action. To act is to take power, to have power, to be powerful. Mutual communication between speakers and listeners is a powerful act.

—Ursula K. Le Guin

---

12. The insight from meditation also gave me an idea of how unsafe other people might feel inside their own heads too, regardless of age or relative position in society. It planted a seed in me of compassion and curiosity toward all people I encounter, including those I do not like or might disregard.

Language is how we make meaning, how we articulate this precious human experience to ourselves and then with others. There are words that consistently stimulate a strong reaction in people. They reveal interesting possibilities and highlight issues of our cultural conditioning. One such word is *conflict*. Because most of us prefer to avoid conflict, and those who bring it, we may find choosing other words to articulate observations or concerns allows people to remain open to hearing us. For example, I might say that *I see a pattern emerging that concerns me*, or inquire *if there is a shared dilemma*. Looking for creative phrasing can help people stay relaxed as we deal with a conflict, instead of freezing—subtly or not—when they hear the word.

Words are walls, or words are windows. To open possibilities, it helps to expand and clarify vocabulary. During exercises on understanding anger, my colleagues and I offered up a wide range of words on an anger continuum: *furious, irritated, tense, irate, aggrieved, outraged, miffed, offended, frustrated.*[13] Then, we conducted a series of exercises that guided participants in playing with and expanding their anger vocabulary. The play is important—fun and levity create room for learning even with challenging topics. Growing our vocabulary for anger and other challenging emotions is like upgrading from a box of eight crayons to a set of sixty-four. It's exciting! Who wants to go back to eight? Having many shades to illustrate how we feel offers increased clarity in understanding and communicating challenging experiences.

A window helps us see the world. All cultures frame worldviews in certain ways. By experimenting with language, we can perceive what exists beyond our conditioned confines. Think about the discussion of pronouns. Beyond the binary framework of she/her/hers and he/him/his, friends who define gender differently inspire with creative language to affirm individual identity.[14] In *Braiding Sweetgrass,* author Robin Wall Kimmerer says we need new pronouns for nature. Rather than using the objectifying word "it," she suggests "ki" for singular and "kin" for plural to honor the living beings of animals, plants, and ecosystems.

Another way that words can better serve values is to distinguish *who people are from what they do.* When people asked about my profession, I didn't

---

13. I am thankful to BayNVC colleague Meganwind Eoyang for introducing me to the anger continuum and for many other pieces of wisdom.
14. For more on the history and variety of gender pronouns, check out https://uwm.edu/lgbtrc/support/gender-pronouns/.

say, "I am the director of the Gandhi Institute." Instead, I said, "I *served* as the director of the Gandhi Institute." It's what I did, not who I am. Remembering this truth connects me to awareness of privilege and to our underlying shared humanity. When my language subtly frames myself and others as being important or unimportant, I lose out and so do they.

Marshall Rosenberg inspired this awareness, especially the use of the verb "to be." Describing people, including myself, by what we do (active and current language) rather than by what we are (static labels) gives breathing space in our identities. It includes choice and infers action. I am not only a writer, or a teacher. I play with my dog, commune with a favorite oak tree daily, watch basketball games with my husband, read voraciously, care for my parents, meditate in the mornings with coffee and inspiring texts. All of this helps me to remember that other people are just as beautifully complex.

Active language helps to avoid seeing others through the lens of fixed judgments. I find it vitally important to say, "She is acting like a jerk," vs. "She is a jerk." The language sets the stage within to extend grace to others, and humility toward myself—sometimes I act like a jerk too! It helps me to remember how dynamic all of us truly are, and that all fixed ideas I hold about another are inherently incomplete or outdated.

From this applied insight we can begin to see Nonviolent Communication as an awareness discipline rather than a communication process. While this practice may seem a mild one at first glance, it's quite a (r)evolutionary one to embrace consistently. Language creates barriers, and knocks them down.

Choosing language consciously and with love is a powerful form of nonviolence. Begin by noticing the violence of many everyday expressions (e.g. shoot you an email; take a stab at that; attack a problem or illness). Monitoring and removing violent metaphors is part of building an awareness discipline. Over time we can become more conscious communicators and celebrate that speech we later regret is far less common.

Your Turn: Think of some labels you apply to yourself in static language. How does it feel to transform them using action language? What common violent metaphors do you notice?

Life Is a Learning Laboratory

Curiosity will conquer fear even more than bravery will.
—James Stephens

Each morning, I start the day reading, writing, reflecting and thanking creation for the gift of another day. I spend time with the thoughts of those who walked this path ahead of me: Howard Thurman, Dr. Martin Luther King Jr., Pema Chodron, Alice Walker, Eknath Easwaran, and many others. I dwell in inspiration with people who help me see more deeply. For more than thirty years, this rhythm has anchored my life and supports my remembering of what matters most each day. I turn up the volume on my intuition. I use that time to surface amends I want to offer for speech and choices that I now regret. Then, I try to bring that spirit into the rest of my day. Much of what follows are the fruits of this practice.

Life is a learning laboratory. It's a place to observe, make mistakes, and discover the operating principles of the world—and of ourselves. One of the most useful studies I've ever undertaken is getting acquainted with the odd and wonderful ways that humans process information. Here are a few of my favorite factoids: we remember information best when embedded in a narrative; we focus on individual actions and overlook systemic and environmental factors; the vast majority of our decisions are made below the level of conscious awareness, especially when we are stressed or tired.[15] On a daily basis, this knowledge helps me be gentle with myself and others.

From efforts to transform my habits, like the work of communication described in the previous section, and time with thousands of people in learning spaces, one pattern I've noticed is how swiftly many of us use new ideas against ourselves. Pretty frequently, when we learn something eye-opening, we start beating ourselves up for our previous ignorance. Perhaps the energy generated by internal judgments like "I should have known that," helps somehow to "glue" new learning into place. It seems that after age three or four, new ideas become instantly packaged in this "should" wrapping paper. No wonder learning can transform from a delight to a chore as we age!

---

15. Numerous scholars and studies have documented that the majority of information and decision making takes place below the surface of conscious awareness. *Thinking, Fast and Slow* by Daniel Kahnemann is one resource that helped me integrate this awareness and others named above.

We can challenge this tendency to dread learning new ideas by seeking to become experts at being amateurs, strengthening the habit of observation. We can benefit from this mindset and the corresponding ability to take things less personally, even ourselves. Observation opens up that all-important space between stimulus and response. That gap becomes familiar terrain, a space to return to and rely upon, a place where creativity lives. In it, we can replace judgments of ourselves and others with empathy, and then apply curiosity.

Gandhi was a dedicated observer. It was the first step in campaigns he participated in, often for long months.[16] Dr. Bernard Lafayette also utilized observation and careful relationship building before and during organizing a 1963 voter registration campaign in Selma, Alabama. Lafayette was observing power dynamics in the community, especially between racial groups and with law enforcement, and he built relationships both with Black leaders and law enforcement. His book detailing those efforts is a tremendous resource as a historic record and as a model for thoughtful organizing in dangerous circumstances.[17]

Curiosity is a meta-skill for practicing nonviolence. It helps connect us to humility and relaxed awareness of our limits. If I stumble into a situation lacking curiosity, it's a warning light flashing, signaling low internal resources, that it's time to replenish and pay attention to what is missing.

Your turn: What natural curiosity do you carry about yourself and the world? Where do you delight in being a perpetual learner?

Permission to Change

As you know, the stakes are much higher for people in the public eye to admit errors. In the decades since his death, Gandhi's character and choices have been questioned, as have Dr. Martin Luther King Jr.'s. Every leader will face criticisms and concerns. Critiques offer a chance to walk the talk of nonviolence. These interactions stir deep questions, such as: can someone be a hero and still be acknowledged as imperfect? Why do we require perfection from people who inspire us? Who benefits, and who is harmed, when heroes are held to such standards? How does demanding perfection disempower us from changing when we learn new information?

16. Joan Bondurant, *Conquest of Violence: The Gandhian Philosophy of Conflict.*
17. Bernard Lafayette Jr., *In Peace and Freedom: My Journey In Selma.*

A critique that directly related to the Institute's values and work regarded the persistent allegations that Gandhi acted in racist ways. During a visit to Phoenix Ashram outside Durban, South Africa, a young Black colleague and I spoke with Ela Gandhi about it. Ela, a social activist and lifelong resident of South Africa, is one of Mohandas Gandhi's grandchildren and sister to Arun Gandhi. We asked her about the reports and charges made against Gandhi over his use of racist language in relation to Black South Africans. Ela, and later Arun, both spoke of their grandfather's emphasis on lifelong learning, humility, and critical self-reflection. The language he used in his early days in South Africa has been rightfully criticized. He absorbed racist attitudes toward himself and toward other People of the Global Majority during his childhood in India and later while in school in England. (**Global Majority** is a collective term for ethnic groups which constitute approximately 85 percent of the global population, used as an alternative to terms which are seen as racialized like "ethnic minority" and "person of color.")[18]

Though he did not use words we would use today, Gandhi described his own internalized racism and the pain it caused in his autobiography. He lived in South Africa for twenty-one years. Over time, Gandhi increasingly recognized how much he and other South Asian people had in common with Black South Africans. He allied with Black people in meaningful ways, from treating wounded Zulus during his medical ambulance service in the Boer War (over British South African objections) to public support for African nations emerging from colonialism, to meetings with African Americans seeking to apply nonviolent methods, such as his 1936 meeting with Sue Bailey and Howard Thurman.

Gandhi published his autobiography in 1925 at the height of his prominence in India, during the years he was becoming a global figure. It is an amazingly transparent book for a leader of his time in relation to mistakes he had made and still sets a high bar for leaders in terms of owning their mistakes, struggles, and shortcomings.[19]

Even for those of us without worldwide fame, old answers can challenge our humility and willingness to work to seek new answers. All of us

18. Gratitude to Dr. Roxanne Manning for introducing me to this term.
19. I wonder about the fury of the attacks on Gandhi, a Person of the Global Majority who stood for the power of nonviolence in the hearts of millions for decades. The tarnishing of his name supports those who seek to gain and keep power via fear and violence. I wonder about the source and energy of some of the attacks.

struggle to own past ignorance, inexperience, and misperceptions. Some of the most critical work in white accountability spaces I lead is to strengthen the capacity for recognizing and acting on new understandings. We can mourn past limitations, celebrate learning, and seek support to integrate, then act from a continuously updating and yet always incomplete understanding of life.

Your turn: Think of a time you changed your mind on a subject. What supported your capacity to open to new thinking? What habits of mind could help you to remain open to questioning beliefs?

"I Am Sophia Auld"—The Importance of Others' Gaze

Existentially, how can I know who I am without others? Our inward and outward gazes are filtered by our eyes, brain, and conditioning. Birds and butterflies see an additional color that humans do not. We will never perceive the ultraviolet that informs their world. Dolphins and bats "see" the sound shapes of sonar and echolocation. Their vision maps us, knowing a human being as the aberration in the way sound moves.

While I don't see in the way that these other creatures can, I can choose to recognize and overcome the limitations of the way my brain and conditioning function. Because **racism** ("a system of advantage based on race," according to Beverly Daniel Tatum[20]) is a root cause *and* an accelerant of violence internally, interpersonally, nationally, and internationally, we can focus on recognizing and excavating the harm of racism within us as a first step. For me, that means continuously asking how, as a white woman, can I learn to transcend my racialized identity, culture, and perspectives?

The urgency of answering that question increased after I read Frederick Douglass's *Narrative of the Life of Frederick Douglass, an American Slave* and his acute observations of white behavior—especially the consequences of whites living with the terrible and corrupting power of legal slavery. The section that cornered my conscience in powerful ways included twelve-year-old Douglass's experience of meeting Sophia Auld. Auld was a white woman without experience of slavery. She had recently married the man who enslaved Douglass. Initially, Sophia Auld treated Douglass like a child

---

20. Beverly Daniel Tatum, *Why Are All the Black Kids Sitting Together in the Cafeteria?: And Other Conversations About Race*, 7.

in her home, instead of a thing. This treatment was shocking to Douglass. He had never experienced humanity from a white person before. Auld taught young Frederick his letters and was chastised by her husband for doing so. In the months that followed, Frederick Douglass watched the system of slavery work on Auld:

"I was utterly astonished at her goodness. She was entirely unlike any other white woman I had ever seen. The crouching servility, usually so acceptable a quality in a slave, did not answer when manifested toward her. Her favor was not gained by it; she seemed to be disturbed by it. . . . Her face was made of heavenly smiles, and her voice of tranquil music. But alas! This kind heart had but a short time to remain as such. The fatal poison of irresponsible power was already in her hands, and soon commenced its infernal work. That cheerful eye, under the influence of slavery, soon became red with rage; that voice, made all of sweet accord, changed to one of harsh and horrid discord; and that angelic face to that of a demon."[21]

On my desk, a sticky note I wrote after reading Douglass catches my eye every day:

I am Sophia Auld

It is a reminder of the unconsciousness that I carry. It brings to mind the responsibility for learning and the unimaginable loss every one of us experiences living in a society steeped in racism. It connects me to mercy for the people of all ages and backgrounds who have been taught to dehumanize—people who have become as lost as Sophia Auld, under the influence of the "fatal poison of irresponsible power."

To challenge my privilege, I seek ways to learn from the gaze of people who are unlike me in race, ethnicity, religion, life experience, and first language through talks, lectures, podcasts, op-eds, and articles. I prioritize volunteer work and relationships that support this commitment. Because I'm a reader, memoirs and biographies help, especially reading about Black women who struggled and triumphed despite the twin harms of racism and sexism. I recommend Keisha N. Blaine's terrific biography of civil rights

---

21. Frederick Douglass, *Narrative of the Life of Frederick Douglass, an American Slave*, 35.

activist Fannie Lou Hamer, *Until I Am Free,* as well as a much earlier book, Harriet Jacobs's *Incidents in the Life of a Slave Girl.* Her book conveys the particular harm that enslaved women dealt with, including bearing children to men who brutalized them and their children. (And while we are on the topic of challenging privilege, it's worth asking why Frederick Douglass's book is so widely known, while Jacobs's equally amazing story of escape and reclaiming her life is not.)

Anti-racism educators like psychologist Dr. Ken Hardy urge us white people to undertake the critical task of developing a thicker skin on the topic of racism, to engage in the work of dismantling the attitudes, systems, and structures of racism.

I call myself a recovering racist. And even with a supportive community, recognizing the past and ongoing pain of racism and the role of white people can be devastating. Although I know that this system is not my fault or the fault of most other white people alive now, I also know that as white people we—like Sophia Auld—benefit. My conditioned response to that complexity is to blame myself and others.

That blame doesn't get us very far in addressing the problem. From learning about violence and about systems, I recognize racism as a fundamental root cause *and* an outcome of violence. That means undoing racism and other intersectional harms offers a genuine lever for change. So I strive to reserve my fury and my energy for changing systems, rather than blaming individuals, and seek ways to fuel this commitment with energy other than blame or shame.

Your Turn: What prompts you to reflect on your identity? What value might there be in recognizing the implicit conditioning you received on how to react and relate to other people?

Humility and Gaps in Perception

Search others for their virtue, and yourself for your vices.
—R. Buckminster Fuller

Reflecting on his years of supporting international philanthropic efforts, leadership expert Robert Greenleaf once said, "I see no middle ground between arrogance and humility." After thinking that over, I see it differently— more like a spectrum with low self-esteem on one end, arrogance at the other, and humility in the middle. It takes self-confidence to be truly humble. Without confidence, humility could be a version of self-effacement—a reflection of low self-esteem. On the other hand, without humility, high self-esteem can veer into arrogance.

Finding this balance requires awareness of our perceptual gaps. It's difficult to see them—like trying to tell the color of your eyes without a mirror. There is one thing that invariably reveals them, however: feedback that is tough to hear. If the information challenges you or makes you uncomfortable, there's a good chance that a perception gap just came into view. Congratulations!

Here's an example of one of my perceptual gaps coming into focus. In 2011, I took the Harvard Implicit Bias Test to measure my internalized racism. This free online test indicated that I had some moderate racial bias. (I define **bias** as mainly unconscious favoritism toward some individuals and groups, and mainly unconscious negativity toward other individuals and groups.) I felt relieved and dismayed, simultaneously. I had felt the bias in me and was glad to be diagnosed with a mild case. And, I would have loved to have had the work I had been doing on myself clear me of it completely. As I grappled with that emotional mix, my youngest daughter was peering over my shoulder, reading the screen. "How can you be racially biased?" she asked, "Look at your work! Look at your friends!" I shook my head and responded, "I grew up in this racially-biased culture and hyper-segregated community.[22] I have internalized countless messages in regards to race."

Although it's painful to acknowledge bias, it's important to remember that none of us choose to receive this conditioning. It was "downloaded" into our brains, starting in childhood, without our consent. Regardless of intelligence, values, or education, it affects each of us. Transforming bias requires us to recognize and to excavate it. Recently I worked with a white woman in conflict with her Black manager. She felt that the examples of biased behavior that her supervisor named were inaccurate because she (the white woman) had been learning about racism and was no longer biased. I

22. https://www.ncbi.nlm.nih.gov/pmc/articles/PMC4886656/

suggested that a different conclusion from her studies could be to assume and accept the inevitability of bias in her thoughts and actions.

To sustain the effort of challenging our biases, we can work to build a healthier, stronger self-identity. We will continue to make mistakes and hopefully learn. We can grieve the ongoing consequences of racism and other forms of bias in our communities and country, from hate crimes to mass shootings, while staying focused on uprooting the causes within ourselves.

Your Turn: What/who/where grounds you? Your answers will offer support during difficult times. If your identity grounds you, use it to learn about being rooted in something. If your relationship(s) ground you or your beliefs offer a sense of rootedness, same thing. Keep looking and updating those perspectives.

Reclaiming Identity

We have stopped caring for one another; we have forgotten that we belong to one another, and that we are responsible for one another's well-being. This forgetting has become a very real threat to our survival as human beings.

—Sherri Mitchell

Growing up with mostly Irish ancestry and not too proud of it (though never sure why), I scorned St. Patrick's Day. I saw it as a day of being embarrassed about Irish roots, with a focus on drinking that felt uncomfortably close to home given my family history of alcoholism. The day feels important in a different way now because, like many white people who have been here for more than two generations, I grew up not experiencing myself as having an ethnic identity. White was normalized—people of different skin tones and races were the ones with an identity. This notion engendered a sense of unexamined numb comfort, until I began to think about race and ethnicity.

White privilege shelters white people from having to deal with the biological myths and social realities of race from the time we are tiny. We get to choose to think about it later in life—or to avoid engaging with it altogether. In the construction of whiteness, connection to homelands and ancestral cultures were sacrificed for the comfort of belonging to the privileged group. As I learned about racism, the history and the living influence of it, I began to have cultural envy and identity *discomfort*.

To face this discomfort head-on, I am very fortunate to have taken a solo trip to Ireland in 2015, and another in 2021. They were journeys intended in part to discover, as Malidoma Patrice Somé says in his book *Rituals*, the indigenous person within each of us—in this case, me. Despite the fact that I live on the land of the Haudenosaunee Confederacy, their rituals are not mine. And regardless of the beauty I may find in aspects of other world cultures, their rituals are not mine either. I wanted to explore what my indigenous roots looked like.

In 2015, I visited Newgrange, a five-thousand-year-old site in the ancient Boyne Valley. Each year, the interior of this large structure is illuminated to its core very briefly and precisely by the rays of the rising sun on December 21, the winter solstice. The effort and the knowledge required to construct such a structure boggles my mind. Whatever the intentions of those early people, for me it represented how important it is to remember and celebrate that there is light in even the darkest times.

Early Celtic people, my ancestors, did not separate spirituality from nature or from everyday life. They saw it as an unbroken whole. I seek that wholeness for myself. During that trip and since, it has felt joyful to find that those roots are refreshing my ongoing self-definition.

In 2021, I visited County Clare, Ireland. Two of my great-grandparents were born just north of the city of Ennis and so it holds my most concentrated connection to ancestral places. I went barefoot frequently, to feel and wonder what it would be like to live where my feet were deeply welcomed—not places, however beloved here, taken through genocide, ethnic cleansing,[23] theft, and broken agreements with indigenous people.

For more than ten years, I have participated in and led groups of white people seeking to become accountable for our deeply uneven share of privileges. Learning alongside others strengthens my capacity to stand for the values I was taught as a child, of liberty and justice for all. Because of these groups and because of what I've learned from reading and travels, I feel more positively connected to other white people. This helps me in

23. https://en.wikipedia.org/wiki/Sullivan_Expedition

the conflict work I do, and in connecting to white friends and family with whom I do not agree. It also helps me as a collaborator with indigenous colleagues—I bring less insecurity and less of a deficit mindset regarding my identity to our important work together.

If you are looking to explore your heritage, intuition is a useful guide. Listen to which parts of your bloodline speak to you, and lean into that. We can also offer attention and gratitude to aspects of our identity that come from soul lineages, via the teachers and teachings that matter to us. Developing a relationship with all these parts of ourselves offers a powerful strategy for stability, insight, and healing.[24]

Belonging is linked to survival at a deep level. If you are not sure what roots you and helps you to belong, keep looking. In the words of restorative practices elder Kay Pranis, "We must create opportunities for belonging that are consistent with our best selves."[25]

Your Turn: Where do you feel most welcome? Which places, people, communities, and rituals strengthen your sense of belonging, growth, and accountability? How do you stay in an ongoing relationship with these places, communities, and rituals to keep the connections refreshed?

Chapter Two Key Ideas

- The work we do not only builds something in the community, it also builds something within us.
- Our words can limit or expand understanding. Conscious communication helps to remove barriers to understanding and reduces violence in our language.
- Observing, making mistakes, and discovering operating principles are important to growing our understanding. Curiosity allows us to identify and address changes with humility and empathy for ourselves and others.
- Accepting past limitations, celebrating learning, and integrating/acting from new information are key to growth.
- Acknowledging privilege and unfair advantage is painful. Blaming and shaming individuals (including ourselves) for systemic problems

---

24. Gratitude to Francis Weller and colleagues for leading a grief ritual leadership training that helped to shape this insight and others in this book.
25. Kay Pranis, *The Little Book of Circle Processes: A New/Old Approach to Peacemaking.*

is counterproductive. Focus that energy instead on learning to create systemic change.

- Perceptual gaps uphold unconscious bias. Building a strong self-identity can strengthen us for the ongoing efforts required to recognize and excavate bias.
- Connecting with heritage and identity grounds human beings to more effectively address harm and inequity.

Chapter Three
A New Way

See, I am doing a new thing
Now it springs up; do you not perceive it?
I am making a way in the desert
and streams in the wasteland

—Isaiah 43:19

Think Before Reacting

Between stimulus and response there is a space. In that space is our power to choose our response. In our response lies our growth and our freedom.

—Viktor Frankl

The fertile potential of nonviolence lives in the gap between stimulus and response. It's the place where we can break the cycle of violence and discover other options. It's where we can change our habitual reactions toward responses more aligned with our values. By pausing, we have a chance to respond with curiosity, deep listening, or to articulate our thoughts and perspective.

Several years ago, a group of high school students in Rochester, New York, launched a club with the support of M. K. Gandhi Institute staff. They called it *Project Think Before Reacting*. In it, the students practiced finding that gap. Club activities focused on knowing how to respond when a friend sends a drama-infused text or when someone makes a joke at their expense in the cafeteria. It gives them the ability to find options with higher potential gains (resolving the problem, keeping their cool, repairing a friendship) and fewer negative consequences (suspension, getting in a fist fight, expulsion). As adults, we need this kind of practice too.

You can start by finding something that helps you notice this gap, and practice every day. Deep breaths, prayer, mantra, songs, poems—use whatever works for you. Try it out not only when you're stressed, but also in response to "good" or "neutral" things. One person I know takes a breath before hitting the send button on her emails. It's a frequent reminder to *think before reacting*.

By practicing, we build the mental muscles into a reflex that kicks into gear when we need it most. If this sounds similar to kung fu, it's because it is. Kazu Haga, nonviolence trainer and author of *Healing Resistance*, likens nonviolence to a martial art—we grow stronger through the practice. Eventually, in a moment of need, thinking before reacting *becomes* our automatic response.

One powerful illustration of this practice paying off occurred at an inter-faith gathering just days after the tragic events of September 11, 2001. Our city was a few hours away from New York City; many local emergency responders were there to offer aid. High levels of fear raced through many people. As faith leaders and activists, we were concerned about the backlash against Muslims. We met at the Islamic Center to collectively mourn, in solidarity with the local Muslim community. I have a vivid memory of that feeling in the room when, in response to a heartfelt question of how best to respond to that painful moment, Islamic Center of Rochester leader Dr. Muhammad Shafiq paused and then said: "People of faith, cool down and get humble."

This simple, powerful advice worked in that moment of extreme tension, and it works now. All of us—whether or not we consider ourselves people of faith—can learn to pause and center instead of responding with a knee-jerk reaction. In that space, a wiser response often emerges.

Your Turn: Take a moment to recognize what helps you to refrain from reacting, and appreciate yourself for all the times you have used that strategy rather than lashing out. What supports you to slow down in a reactive moment? What benefits result from this effort?

Uprooting Contempt

Human beings will never be convinced by other human beings who try to humiliate them. In nearly every case, such condemnation only reinforces the behavior it is trying to end. When people are accused of acts they know they are guilty of by people who hold them in contempt, they almost always retreat even further into their self-destructive behavior. If they do change, it is from fear, or perhaps hypocrisy, but not from their own truth.
—Andrew Harvey

We have no morally persuasive power for those who can feel our underlying contempt.
—Dr. Martin Luther King Jr.

As we explore the gap between stimulus and response, we might feel contempt bubbling up, especially for our past gaps in understanding. Contempt is the feeling that a person or a thing is beneath consideration, worthless, or deserving scorn. In many contexts, it is a gateway to lasting harm.[26] Contempt sets the table for dehumanizing self and others, for creating, among other things, what Marshall Rosenberg called enemy images.[27] We may experience enemy images as static judgments of ourselves and others that block us from a more complete, and more compassionate, understanding. Examples of enemy images at work might include fixed narratives about who's a good worker, who's responsible, who deserves support and who does not.

If you grew up in an alcoholic family system, like I did, you may have seen the destruction caused by contempt and enemy images. Knowing the destructive power of both, I take time to recognize and dismantle the presence of contempt and enemy images when they show up. I do this by paying attention to where my empathy does not flow, by noticing stories that I have that are fixed rather than fluid, by seeking to transform anger rather than holding on to it and feeding it, and by grieving the gap between what is happening and what I wish was happening. We will go into detail about these approaches in this chapter.

Refusal to host contempt and enemy images offers a protective factor for my wholeheartedness and peace of mind, as contempt feels corrosive to my spirit. I believe it is similarly corrosive for all of us. Developing the capacity to notice and refrain from giving into contempt helps me out in many ways: as a leader, a colleague, a conflict resolver, a friend, a spouse.

Thanks to television and social media, we now have tremendous amounts of information of the kind that Howard Thurman called "contact without fellowship."[28] We are exposed to information about others without knowing the full picture or having a relationship that calls on us to grow in understanding of one another, at a speed that further diminishes connection.[29]

In *Systems Thinking for Social Change,* author David Peter Stroh maintains that conflict without contempt is essential for system change—in families, groups, and organizations. Those who hold power (e.g. a parent, teacher, or manager) must be able to listen and learn from those who are not served by the system—whether it's a family, a classroom, a department, or

26. https://crab.rutgers.edu/users/roseman/Roseman.2018.RejectingTheUnworthy-TheCauses ComponentsAndConsequencesOfContempt.pdf
27. https://www.nonviolentcommunication.com/resources/articles-about-nvc/transforming-enemy-images/
28. Howard Thurman, *Jesus and the Disinherited.* MLK is said to have carried this book with him in the last years of his life. One of my most influential books!
29. https://www.rochester.edu/newscenter/study-of-headlines-shows-media-bias-growing-563502/

an organization—without blame and without contempt. Since it is easy to disregard people who have less power than us, we may be prone to feeling defensive or irate when questioned. Recognizing that our positionality limits our understanding, we can challenge ourselves to welcome divergent voices (which doesn't mean we won't need to take a deep breath first).

Understanding contempt as a way to feel more powerful can help us to understand why it is so pervasive:

> Feeling contempt asserts power or status. Therefore, those who are uncertain about their status may be more likely to manifest contempt to assert their superiority over others. In that way, sometimes people in "subordinate" positions may feel contempt towards those who have a higher social, political, or legal ranking. Some examples include the potential contempt teenagers may feel towards adults, workers for their bosses, or prisoners for their guards. While this kind of "upward contempt" is common, the reverse can also be true in which someone with a higher ranking may feel contempt towards those with a lower ranking.[30]

Upward contempt relates to the notion of empathy not flowing well "uphill," to the ease of dehumanizing people that we envy or resent. When contempt is present, everybody loses out.

Your turn: What stimulates contempt in you, at work and elsewhere? Notice when and where this happens. How much choice do you have over your thoughts and speech when feelings of contempt occur? What would it cost you to let go of contempt? How might it benefit you?

Empathy Doesn't Flow Uphill

The secret to success is not the absence of failure, but the absence of envy.
—Herodotus

Empathy doesn't flow uphill. We can see examples of this everywhere, from our social circles to the way society treats celebrities: beauty, fortune, power, and fame are more likely to provoke envy than empathy. It's easier to find compassion for people who struggle and those who face challenges, heavy discrimination, or major setbacks. Care seemingly flows more slowly, if at

---

30. https://www.paulekman.com/universal-emotions/what-is-contempt/

all, towards those we see as having more. Pause for a moment and check—does this fit with your experience?

The people I most often resent are those I perceive as having more power than me. Sometimes this dynamic exists with people remote from me, like politicians, and sometimes with those I worked for or learned from. Finding ways to become free of resentment toward those I perceive as holding structural power is one of the fruits of my nonviolence practice. These are individuals whose decisions affect others through their role, influence, or wealth—public officials, presidents of universities, chairpersons of banks and foundations, celebrities, etc.

Here is a strategy to become free of this particular flavor of resentment. While relating to people in those positions, imagine the isolation they may feel. The more social or structural power an individual seemingly has, the less they may be seen as a human being, and the less honesty they receive. Several years ago, I spoke in Pittsburgh, Pennsylvania, on the topic of rank and privilege. A man who served for one year as interim director of a large community foundation said that every relationship in his life changed while he occupied that role, except the one with his wife. Even though it was understood that his role was temporary, he was treated as if he suddenly had pearls falling from his lips whenever he spoke. He said he would not have believed it without that experience. Similar dynamics occur with people who possess physical beauty, fame, wealth, and position. Suddenly, they're not ordinary people with insecurities, hidden dreams, and hobbies. They are seen solely as their titles, talents, or money.

With some effort, we can experience benefits—both materially and spiritually—of approaching power holders in an authentic way. It helps us to consciously navigate the uneven power dynamics in the work we do. On a personal note, my commitment to be authentic with power holders was a factor in the close relationship I developed with Nonviolent Communication originator Marshall Rosenberg. He said he could relax with me because I wasn't seeking approval from him.

I have an acquaintance whose family holds enormous wealth. For most people, the mere mention of their last name invokes notions of mansions and private islands. My acquaintance once confessed to me the pain of seeing people's faces change when they learned his identity. (I also felt that change when I heard of his family connection, and both mourned and understood my reaction.) All of us struggle to remember the full humanity of those who we relate to as having more power, rank, and privilege. All of us overlook the power that we hold and are amazed that others at times resent us for having it. We will talk more about the addictive qualities of power and rank in chapter 8.

I strive to remember this insight every day, and to remain aware of the reality that many inevitably struggle to see me and my humanity, for the same reasons. I remain vigilant and therefore more accountable and useful, for the power and rank I have before asking others to do the same.

Your Turn: Who triggers you in their apparent unconsciousness regarding their power? It may be a family member, colleague, or community leader. Can you speak about power differences at work, and be heard and understood? What helps you to retain awareness of the power you have and may overlook?

Living Between Stories

We think we tell stories, but stories often tell us, tell us to love or hate, to see or be seen. Often, too often, stories saddle us, ride us, whip us onward, tell us what to do, and we do it without questioning. The task of learning to be free requires learning to hear them, to question them, to pause and hear silence, to name them, and then become a storyteller.

—Rebecca Solnit

In 2004, I was driving through Oakland, California, listening to a radio interview with author Mary Catherine Bateson. She described living with coexisting, often contradictory narratives and said that which narrative showed up depended on who she was with, how she was feeling, and what she was doing.

Listening to her speak, I realized that I too have a couple narratives running like a low-level radio playing in the background. Depending on who I'm around—and how I'm feeling—I'm listening to one or the other story, tuning into that narrative like talk radio. When I feel good, the "shiny" narrative emerges—the good stuff. "Things are great. I feel hopeful about x, y, and z. We/I can make significant contributions that will make a difference to the future." This also happens when I'm in the presence of someone I don't know well or want to impress. Or sometimes, the shinier narrative emerges when I'm with a younger person and I want to inspire hope.

When my internal resources are low, or when I'm in the company of a sympathetic ear, I switch stations. The narrative that comes to the foreground is the one of discouragement and worries, of challenges, rather than possibilities.

Have you ever experienced anything similar? We can find ourselves steered by these powerful narratives unless we do one important thing: notice. Without awareness, either narrative can swiftly balloon into feeling like our whole reality, forgetting that just a few hours—or moments—ago, we were immersed in a different story. There is power and grace in noticing stories without believing them. I call it *living between stories*. Freeing ourselves from the influence of a single story gives us the perspective needed to see pieces of truth in all narratives, opening us up to more possibilities.

The stories we carry regarding colleagues, projects, and efforts frequently dominate our consciousness and conversations about work.

Growing this awareness can also make us more conscious consumers of media, noticing which stories are fed to us and by whom. When I read or watch mainstream US media, I notice feelings of overwhelm, fear, and frequent fury about what is happening politically, economically, and environmentally. For balance, I make efforts to consume local and alternative media. I read *Yes Magazine* as a resource that highlights innovation and systemic change, the weekly edition of Nonviolence News,[31] and media outside the US to open my perspectives. I learned the importance of disciplined media consumption from conversations with two colleagues from Rwanda who reflected on the role media played to incite genocide there in 1994.[32]

When our thinking is consumed with grief or despair, we can look for the "other narrative" and then attempt to rest between them, like a relaxed spider on her web.

---

31. Please subscribe to and support this project! www.nonviolencenews.org
32. https://kenan.ethics.duke.edu/media-manipulation-suppression-and-the-rwandan-genocide/

From these efforts, I have come to believe that *despair is a form of arrogance*, implying that I somehow know the outcome of a situation when I, of course, cannot. Life is full of surprises and unintended consequences. Since despair is an old companion of mine, this awareness offers me strength and clarity in difficult moments, to question assumptions that seem inevitable when I feel overwhelmed.

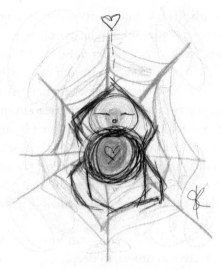

Victor Frankl, psychologist, author, and Holocaust survivor, speaks of despair as "suffering without meaning" and suggests that a way out is to find and increase meaning in our lives.[33] This could take many forms, including at places we volunteer or work. There are a million ways to grow meaning.

Your Turn: Pay attention to who and what stimulates your "single stories," at work and elsewhere. What is your media diet composed of? Where can you look for other potential narratives? Is there an image that appeals to you, like my relaxed spider does to me, that might help you remember the space between?

Suffering: Straw into Gold

Let this darkness be a bell tower
and you the bell. As you ring,
what batters you becomes your strength.

—Rainer Maria Rilke

I have been building a mental rubric of my heroes for years. I track the commonalities they share like courage, compassion, and determination, and rejoice when another common element reveals itself. One of those common elements lies in how my heroes face suffering and give it more meaning, transmuting it from an individual experience to one of universality.

33. "Viktor Frankl on Finding Meaning in Despair," https://www.youtube.com/watch?v=9rYRKZfunJA.

With Arun Gandhi, two young colleagues from the Institute, and several others, I visited the train station platform in Pietermaritzburg where, just one week after arriving in South Africa in 1893, Mohandas Gandhi was kicked off a train for refusing to comply with racial segregation. He spent a cold night shivering on a bench, thinking. During those hours, he made an important moral imaginative leap from outrage regarding his own situation to the widespread injustice faced by all Indians living in South Africa. Instead of dwelling on his discomfort, he started thinking systemically about the problem, which meant the solution would not just benefit him— it would have to help them all. Later, he would describe that miserable night as one of the transformative moments of his life.

Every kind of suffering can serve as a doorway through which to see ourselves in others, to deeply experience our shared humanity. If your colleagues disappoint or your lover breaks your heart, if the photo of a baby in a war zone haunts your thoughts, or the refusal of leaders to lead or appear to care creates outrage in you, use all of it as fuel. Throw your heartbreak into the furnace of your fierce love. Use that transformed energy like a power plant for your efforts toward justice. If you use suffering in this way—rather than letting it simmer or become blame, rage, and bitterness—you may discover the ability to generate non-toxic, renewable energy for your life.

In nonviolence, suffering is neither caused, nor sought out, *nor avoided*. In the context of social change, Gandhi, King, Abdul Ghaffar Khan, James Lawson, and others have reflected on the willingness to endure suffering as essential for change. They made strategic choices to risk pain, hardship, and repression to move humanity closer to freedom and justice. Describing the principles of Kingian nonviolence, Kazu Haga expresses this as "nonviolence asks that we accept suffering . . . *for the sake of the cause* . . . in pursuit of the goal."[34]

Strategic willingness to suffer was a core tenet for Gandhi. As a Hindu, he drew spiritual fortitude from his faith as he persevered through arrests, prison sentences, beatings, hunger strikes, and setbacks. The same is true for Muslims like Khan and the 100,000 members of the world's first non-violent army that he created in what is now Pakistan, who bore extreme suffering at the hands of the British army.[35] The same is true for Dr. King, and thousands of nonviolent participants in the US civil rights movement.

34. Kazu Haga, *Healing Resistance: A Radically Different Response to Harm*, 139.
35. https://www.nonviolent-conflict.org/khudai-khidmatgar-servants-god-movement-bad-shah-khan-northwest-frontier-british-india-1933-1937

For many, their Christian faith offered them a compass for continuing to push for change without reprisal despite bombings, assaults, death threats, jail time, and lynchings. Tens of thousands of people globally have utilized these tactics.

How does bearing suffering in this way effect change? It has been shown to create a transformative atmosphere for those who participate, it awakens admiration and reluctance to harm on behalf of those who are being paid to oppress and harm, and it seizes the moral advantage in the conflict. Practically, it's a good strategy as few non-state actors can match the weaponry and capacity to commit violence that governments possess.[36]

When several Tibetan monks visited a youth project in Rochester, New York, they illustrated how influential upbringing and cultural background are in shaping our experience of and response to suffering. During their visit, they participated in a dialogue with young men who had grown up in Rochester. Each group reflected on the violence they had personally experienced: the Rochester youth discussed loss, murder, and discrimination, and the visiting monks discussed their loss of freedom, genocide, and immolation. While their painful experiences were similar, the resulting feelings were starkly different: the Rochester youth expressed feeling anger, hopelessness, and sadness; the monks, surprisingly, reported feeling compassion, forgiveness, and even happiness.[37]

Feeling sad and angry is a natural response to pain. So how did these monks arrive at happiness? The monks drew from their culture and religious training to transcend suffering. While they may have still felt anger or grief, their religion and culture helped them discover how to transform suffering from straw into gold in their lives.

Whether we're trying to navigate painful experiences or confronting suffering as we push for change at work and elsewhere, transforming what the world hurls at us is a superpower we can cultivate. To paraphrase Howard Thurman, we must learn to handle suffering, or be handled by it. Uncountable hardships are happening all around: friends and family die, people lose jobs and homes, wars break out, pandemics erupt. Every one of them is an opportunity to practice finding ways to make sense of suffering, building our skills for wholehearted living.

---

36. Erica Chenoweth, *Civil Resistance: What Everyone Needs to Know.*
37. Thanks to Professor Tim Weider for permission to share this story and for his beautiful work.

Your Turn: Have there been times in your life when you were willing to experience suffering? It may be a physical workout to increase endurance, care for a family member, or work that places you at your growing edge. What gifts have you received from those experiences?

Heartbreak as a Power Plant

William Blake said, "The deeper the sorrow, the greater the joy." When we send our grief into exile, we simultaneously condemn our lives to an absence of joy.
—Francis Weller

Transforming suffering matters because unexpressed sorrow clogs emotional arteries. If we don't deal with it, it spills out onto others, often in harmful ways. We may be wrestling with personal sorrow, like losing a loved one, or despair at the state of the world, or the quiet desperation of unfulfilled dreams. Or, our grief may be collective sorrow, such as mourning a mass shooting, war, climate change, or devastating disaster. Whatever the source, grief can affect every part of our lives. Relating to it consciously is essential if we wish to transform rather than transfer grief and suffering onto others.

The first step in transforming suffering is to understand our usual response. My early tendency under the influence of grief was to isolate. I remember the day my father died. I was fourteen years old and sought out a corner of the basement in our house, like an animal in a burrow, while the fact of his loss washed over me. I had already inhaled messages that people who cried were not "doing well" and that those who were not "doing well" were "troubled" youth. I felt afraid to be seen that way, so I made sure no one could see me.

I was also taught, somehow, not to cry. Now I worry about how little crying goes on, especially because crying is a bodily function, a release, like urinating. We don't judge ourselves for urinating—or I haven't met anyone yet who admits to it—but we judge ourselves for crying. Why, oh why, do we do that? Our bodies are built to process and release grief through tears. Wouldn't we worry about a baby or toddler who never cried?

My tendencies now are slightly different. In addition to isolating myself, I tend to ignore grief, using busyness as an excuse. And yet, in leadership roles, whether as a parent, supervisor, mentor, or elder, I know what happens when I choose not to acknowledge grief: it builds up and then leaks out in a painful trickle-down effect. When I am stifling sorrow, whether at home or at work, I become brusque, task-oriented, moving fast and furious. Or, I grow distant and disconnected—a stranger to myself and to others, at work and at home.

The following strategies help to compost suffering and grief into faith and love. I write from my lived experience in the hope that these ideas offer support during the inevitable challenges you face too.

- **Grief and your thoughts about your grief are not the same thing. Learn to differentiate.** Grief is a feeling, often unexpected, stimulated by catching sight of something, a memory, or a song. I choose not to override grief as much as possible but to experience it like beautiful, painful weather. Once it passes, in seconds or minutes, I don't hang on by fueling it with thoughts. I let the animal of my attention take me into what is next.
- **Know what offers you solace even on your worst days.** This is unique to each of us. My list includes flowers and green growing things, walking or swimming, petting and singing to my dog, vibrant colors, and young people. What makes you feel willing to remain alive, no matter what?
- **Respect the power of music.** Music is and has been part of human ceremonies in cultures around the world. I have noticed that I often feel emotionally derailed by music. These days I limit listening to music in general and instead use it as a treat for myself.
- **Don't believe your thoughts between the hours of 11 p.m. and 5 a.m.** In those insomniatic bouts, my worries loom large, rearing their heads in overblown ways. If my middle-of-the-night conviction still makes sense at 9 a.m., I pay attention then. (Adjust this to fit your sleep schedule.)
- **When thoughts run wild, discover ways to quiet them.** Memorizing poetry is a strategy I employ, and I then benefit from having poems within for soulful nourishment. When thoughts gnaw at me, I break the cycle by picking up a piece of poetry and find it quiets the pain and cultivates calm.[38] There is something so special about language liberated from the rules of grammar! I like writing poetry too.
- **Talk about what's happening with a trusted person.** Anguish shrinks when accompanied by loving attention.

---

38. There's research on the calming effect of poetry! https://nautil.us/feeling-stressed-read-a-poem-20699/

Your Turn: What are your strategies when faced with suffering and grief? How well do those strategies serve for metabolizing those experiences? Is there a new approach you want to try, from the list above or another source, to build this essential capacity?

Holding Grief with Others

I have seen healing happen through grief circles, holding space for people to speak their truth.

—Jessica, served as board member at the M. K. Gandhi Institute

Where there is sorrow, there is holy ground.

—Oscar Wilde

For almost twenty years, I've organized and hosted space for people to explore grief, from personal pain to world anguish. We've done this work in retreat settings and as a regular event, both in person and online, at the Gandhi Institute. Some of my most treasured relationships were forged in those spaces. Many times, I have witnessed and experienced the transformative energy that waits on the other side of loss and suffering when we grieve with others.

Author and Zen Hospice Project cofounder Frank Ostaseski offers the following formula:

$$\text{Pain} + \text{resistance} = \text{suffering.}$$

He says, "Grief work is in part to melt this resistance to the pain, by easing the suffering and turning pain into what it is meant to be: our great teacher."

The power of cultural conditioning is evident in how difficult it is for many of us to participate in grief work. Our current dominant culture default setting appears to be to ignore grief, to numb out, to let grief emerge when we are alone, or perhaps one-on-one.[39] Though challenging to overcome this pattern, learning to hold grief in groups can be comforting and generative—we remember we are not alone.

---

39. Francis Weller, *The Wild Edge of Sorrow: Rituals of Renewal and the Sacred Work of Grief,* "Chapter 6." Grateful for Weller's framing of collectively living in a "flatline culture—a culture of suppressed emotions," and for his teachings with colleauges on holding grief in community.

When starting a grief group, try what Francis Weller calls "warming up our grief." Picture wading into the water, getting used to the temperature, and maybe taking in the view before swimming. Consider starting with a question like "What feels right about suppressing grief?" to surface the suppression, to acknowledge that grief exists, and to honor the needs met by the strategy of suppression, before asking people to experiment with setting it aside.

Sharing grief with others is a critical life skill. It supports us in responding with resilience to personal losses and to universal events, rather than fighting reality. Most of all, we remember that we are not alone. Regular participation in these practices is part of what I call "grief hygiene." Just as hygiene practices support our physical health, grief hygiene is an important part of managing our mental and emotional health. I can tell I'm overdue when I begin to speak and act from suppressed pain in ways I regret later. I can also tell I am overdue when my heart feels heavy in my chest. I imagine my heart like a sponge—it needs to be wrung out and to dry in the sunshine for a bit to keep doing its job.

At the Gandhi Institute we experiment with different forms for holding grief. Participation is a core practice for my personal grief hygiene. Here is a sample process for weekly online gatherings created during the COVID-19 pandemic:

- Gather for 60 minutes with up to 10 people. Facilitators light a candle (participants, too, if they can) and have some water to sip.
- We begin with some quiet—mindful breath, a body scan, dropping the shoulders—consciously inhabiting our physical selves.
- Next, we do a check-in of 1 minute or less. Participants share their name and whatever they want to say about what brought them to the space. (10 minutes)
- A facilitator or participant shares a reading, song, or poem to support the journey from head to heart. (5 minutes)
- Quiet time for participants to draw, write, meditate, etc. I encourage drawing—especially for people who don't consider themselves "artists"—as a way of accessing other parts of ourselves. This time is focused on process, not on outcomes. (12–15 minutes)
- The group comes together and takes turns sharing whatever they feel willing to. Usually, many types of grief show up. We don't compare or evaluate grief. Sometimes grief over "small" losses compounds from

previous ones. Often, not always, themes of insights and sharing tend to emerge. (20–25 minutes)
- Here are some prompts to support self-connection:
  - What is ending in your life right now? What is just beginning?
  - Today, I am really missing . . .
  - I have been feeling a lot of . . .
  - I feel most connected to my grief when . . .
  - I feel most held in my grief when . . .
  - I can honor my grieving process by . . .
  - I could use more of . . .
  - I could use less of . . .
- Closing round: Ask a question like "What is something you are taking away from our time?" (10 minutes)

These gatherings are designed so that the facilitators participate too. We try to co-facilitate so that if either of us comes with an especially heavy heart, the other can take the lead. If the participant number is higher, check-ins happen in pairs or small groups, and are followed by a collective harvesting of responses. Online, you can use a chat feature for this.

This group processing format can feel unfamiliar to many of us. For others, it's cherished and familiar. For example, from the founding of their 1000-year-old-confederacy, the Haudenosaunee have prioritized transformation by acknowledging and honoring grief as part of leadership transitions.[40] If this type of understanding were present in all cultures' leadership transitions, what benefits would accrue?

When grief is expressed in a group, even when the underlying situation being grieved is unchanged, participants commonly notice relief, love, and even joy rising. I believe this is the release of energy that was being used to keep grief at arm's length. How much insight and energy could be freed to serve life if more of us took on transforming suffering and grief? How much more freedom and courage would we find? How much less fear?

Your Turn: Celebrate spaces in your life where people speak about grief and exchange support. Can you find more ways to metabolize this energy? Can you speak more openly to others, at work and elsewhere, about how they grieve and discover ways you could help one another?

---

40. https://narf.org/nill/documents/peacemaking/2016haudenosaunee-peacemaking.pdf

Understanding Anger

Anger is like a fire. It warms—until it burns. It's illuminating—until it blinds. It seems to give power—until it overpowers. Anger emerges when we feel threatened or powerless.

If you investigate anger in yourself and others, you may notice a common pattern—anger is a secondary response. Its intensity erupts so rapidly that it is easy to miss the presence of the first response: fear. Here's an example I have shared in workshops and talks countless times: A child runs into the street. A car slams on the brakes, nearly hitting them. The parent/older sibling/guardian yanks the child back and yells, "Don't ever do that again!" When I ask for guesses as to what that person may be really feeling, people of all ages immediately name fear. (As I edit this book, a parent told me this exact story, once again! He talked about anger, and said yes when I asked if fear was the underlying fuel.) Almost universally, the lightbulb snaps on. They know—we all know—that the parent sounds angry but is actually terrified, afraid for the safety of the child. Before anger rips through us, our hearts plummet into our guts. Adrenaline whips through our body in a biological reaction to danger. Fear is converted into fuel for action, a mechanism humans have used for hundreds of thousands of years to stay alive.

When a paper mill dumps toxins in the water, when a court strips away human rights, when the economy crashes and elected leaders appear to do nothing . . . anger burns. Beneath that anger is fear: for our health, our safety, our families' survival. It is intimately tied to love. Love for our community, for children. Love for the Earth and for the well-being of the world.

On a smaller scale, this pattern plays out in everyday squabbles and spats. A coworker borrows our stapler and forgets to return it. We snap at them when really we are afraid of being undervalued. Our kids forget their homework and we yell, irritation masking deeper concern for their future.

If anger is a secondary reaction, that means we have a microsecond-long chance to choose the response to our flashpoints of fear and threatened love. In that gap lies the opportunity to think before reacting. Knowing that anger is often prompted by care and concern also allows us to choose to respond to others' anger with more presence and mercy.

Anger is normal. And, as we all know, it frequently doesn't get us what we want. Sometimes, the only person burned by our anger is us. Other times, the brunt of anger is borne by the people around us. Dr. King called nonviolent resistance "released anger under discipline for maximum effect." Whether we're dealing with social injustice or a workplace tiff, nonviolence invites us to explore what awareness, discipline, and skillful releases can do to change the situation.

Since anger is normal and common, we have ample opportunities to get to know it as it arises in us. Study it. What predictably generates anger in you? What are your options once it shows up? My anger flares when my care for something intersects with a sense of helplessness, either from a lack of clarity or a lack of ability to make the change I think is best. What are those flashpoints for you at home, and in places where you work, worship, and volunteer? These places hold people and efforts that matter to us, and therefore naturally generate frustration, impatience, and other shades of anger.

When we are truly angry with another person (not a system), it can help to understand and address the root cause of the issue. The list of universal needs derived from Nonviolent Communication can be used to identify unmet wants and needs. After getting clarity and support, we can do a "social change move": Instead of getting uptight, or using friends to fan the flames of resentment, get curious about what motivated the other person to do what they did. If you're not yet able to be curious, apply more understanding, time, and empathic connection until you regain interest in what motivated the other. A sense of inquiry rather than judgment indicates that you're ready to speak with the other person in ways that might help resolve the dispute. This is a social change opportunity because most of us have been trained to judge, blame, and distance ourselves from others when we feel angry. Disrupting this pattern is transformative for all.

Please do not misunderstand: anger deserves space for expression. We're not trying to silence it. We're trying to understand it, looking for ways to put more power—not less—into our efforts to learn and grow from challenges, extend mercy, and seek justice. Rather than trying to squelch the presence of anger, we can grow the ability to choose and respond with increasing skill. It's about digging deeper, reclaiming that energy, and unleashing love and care as a force for change. In Cyndi Suarez's words, it is about refusing a powerless identity.[41] In Dr. King's words, it's about finding the strength to love. Understanding our own anger sets us up to be far more useful to others in the grip of their anger, who are quite possibly just as lost or scared or lonely under its influence.

Your turn: What did you learn about anger as a child, from the giants in your life—such as an older sibling, or your mom or dad? Now, where does anger frequently show up, and how do you relate to it when it does? How are feelings related to anger conveyed at work, and how are they dealt with? What's the best use of anger you have witnessed?

Anger: Energy for Action

Using anger intelligently makes life better on a personal basis and a global one too.
—Arun Gandhi

In his books *Legacy of Love* and *The Gift of Anger*, Arun Gandhi shares many memorable stories of living with his grandparents between the ages of twelve and fourteen, amidst the height of Mohandas Gandhi's political career in India. Raised in South Africa, Arun struggled with anger from experiencing and witnessing racial violence. His parents became worried and sent him to live for two years with his grandparents. Gandhi made time every day to teach his grandson, often about emotions like anger. Speaking to Arun, Gandhi used a different metaphor than fire for anger. He compared anger to electricity—a powerful force that can destroy or be harnessed for tremendous good.

A few months after the murder of Trayvon Martin, I was driving past a suburban retail center. On the corner, a Black youth was waiting at a bus stop—an unusual sight in the mostly-white eastern suburbs of Rochester, New York. The bus approached as I idled at the stoplight; it drove past the bus stop where the youth stood and pulled up behind me at the light. The youth came running and knocked on the bus door to be admitted. In my rearview mirror, I watched the white driver shake his head and look away. The youth froze, then ran around and started knocking on the front of the bus, demanding to be admitted.

---

41. Cyndi Suarez, *The Power Manual: How to Master Complex Power Dynamics*, "Section One: Refusing Powerless Identities."

All of this happened in moments. Remembering Trayvon, I became afraid for this young person's safety. The driver could have hit the gas, or called police who may have escalated the situation in other ways.

I jumped from my car and asked if I could give him a ride. At first, in his apparent fury, he wasn't able to hear me. I raised my voice, saying that I was worried about his safety, could I please give him a ride? As we started to drive, he spent five minutes continuing to speak about the unfairness, how he had come out there for a job, and just wanted today to be a good day. I asked a couple of questions, listened, and watched him slowly start to relax. We had a pretty good visit in the time it took to get downtown.

I share this story to illustrate the usefulness of—and imperative need for—learning how to be relaxed in the face of anger. Most white people hold unexamined fear of Black and Brown people. This fear, cultivated by the media and worsened by the scarcity of genuine relationships in hyper-segregated communities like Rochester,[42] is deadly for People of the Global Majority. While I celebrate feeling relaxed and understanding of this youth's anger that day rather than feeling fearful, looking back, I regret that I did not address the systemic issue of the bus driver choosing to drive past the youth. I wish I had gotten the bus number and called the company or supported the youth in taking action. I didn't know enough to think of this. Now, I hope I will have the presence of mind to do more. My response was limited by not thinking systemically.

Similarly, many of us personalize anger toward individuals when that feeling is partly in response to a systemic issue. We think of racist police officers as "bad apples" instead of critically challenging the entire system of policing. We rail against billionaires without objecting to the economic and political structures that supported the accumulation of their wealth. At work, we become angry with a coworker who is not pulling their weight, or who is making biased remarks, instead of asking about the systems in place that offer timely feedback to staff, and support for difficult, necessary conversations.

Understanding the concept of fundamental attribution error can help focus attention on systemic factors while also developing skills for holding courageous difficult conversations. **Fundamental attribution error** is a cognitive attribution bias where observers underemphasize situational and

42. https://belonging.berkeley.edu/most-least-segregated-cities

environmental factors for the behavior of an actor while overemphasizing personality factors.[43] In their book *Switch: How to Change Things When Change Is Hard*, authors Chip and Dan Heath recommend remembering that in these instances you are having a situation problem, not a people problem.

Focusing anger on unjust systems rather than individuals can be overwhelming, *and* can fuel efforts for change. Dr. King tells a poignant story about seeing his father's anger at the system of segregation. As a boy, King's father took him to a shoe store. The salesperson told them to go to the back—away from the whites-only section. King's father took his son by the hand and walked out of the store. "This was the first time I had seen Dad so furious," King later recalled, in a collection of writings called *The Autobiography of Martin Luther King, Jr.* "That experience revealed to me at a very early age that my father had not adjusted to the system, and that played a great part in shaping my conscience."

Though Martin Luther King Sr. had lived his life dealing with segregation, by staying angry and not adjusting he demanded something better. His anger about the way things were prevented him from getting numb and prevented his son from numbly accepting the system he was born into.

Your turn: How does anger toward systemic ills express itself in your life? Do you have spaces to constructively express this care that leads to action? Can you think of a time when you wished you had held a systemic view on a situation, instead of personalizing it by blaming another?

Put On Your Oxygen Mask First

Even a cactus needs sunlight, soil, and a drop of water. Especially if it wants to bloom.

—Rivera Sun

You yourself, as much as anybody in the entire universe, deserve your love and affection.

—Buddha

---

43. https://en.wikipedia.org/wiki/Fundamental_attribution_error

Deeply absorbed in my efforts to relate to anger and suffering in others, to think and apply systemic responses, I found it easy (and habitual) to overlook my own well-being. As an adult, I found that the last part of creation I cared for was, well, me. So I loved hearing Marshall Rosenberg long ago advise people to remember the wisdom of airline personnel. If you have had the privilege to fly on an airplane, you have heard it too: In case of an emergency, everyone is asked to place oxygen masks on themselves before assisting other passengers.

Take your own physical, emotional, and spiritual sustenance seriously. Notice what lowers your resilience and attend to it. Everyone benefits when you do. For those whose familial and professional focus is on serving others, look at it this way: Nourishing yourself allows you to be more useful. Rather than pretending, you may build the capacity to be fully present.

In the middle of writing this, my stepdad bellows, "Your mom fell!" Once again, I race down the stairs to help my eighty-five-year-old mother, leaving an unfinished sentence on this page. No matter what she's got going on, my mom will be better off if I take a microbreak—a few deep breaths—before I get to her. So will I. Putting on the oxygen mask doesn't necessarily take much, and it's vital to me for being truly useful.

I resist the idea of needing support. Somewhere, I picked up the idea that instead of needing help, I should constantly offer it to others. Sound familiar? We learn it in story and school, culture and society, religious doctrine and pop culture. *Weak people need help; strong people help others.* In my head, I want to be as low-maintenance as a cactus and as self-contained as a spaceship, even when I know intellectually that humans aren't designed that way. We all benefit from nourishment, chances to recharge and recover, and ongoing support. Since this superhero delusion seems to be a near-universal ailment, I try not to be hard on myself for falling for it. Learning about the attributes of white supremacy culture helped me recognize that individualism, going it alone, is my deeply-embedded default setting.[44] (We will discuss more about the attributes of white supremacy culture in chapter 5.)

There's a phrase from Alcoholics Anonymous that says, "The phone weighs a hundred pounds when we most need to pick it up to ask for help." Recent research backs this understanding.[45] Knowing this, I have set thirty-minute

---

44. https://www.whitesupremacyculture.info
45. https://www.sciencedirect.com/science/article/pii/S0191308518300054

conversations every week with various friends. I learned this invaluable practice from a leadership program, and from my friend Miki Kashtan. The time is an exchange of support for challenges, and for sharing celebrations as fuel for the journey. I use it as a space to prepare for and recover from difficulties. Since beginning this practice years ago, I notice a higher degree of resilience in myself.

Creating a framework of support also includes everyday rituals. Earlier, I mentioned my treasured morning quiet time. In this contemplative space, I breathe, read, write, and then take a walk. Life is anchored and enriched through this rhythm. Facilitating and attending regular grief circles sets a rhythm for releasing accumulated stress and losses. Rituals and rhythms—such as pausing to check in before conversations or meetings begin, or caring for plants—can support us at work too. At the Institute, taking breaks by tending to the space, inside or out, offers centering moments for all the staff.

Prayer, walks, meditations, or a favorite quote can be used throughout our days to stay connected to the wellspring of inner nourishment. Whatever creative shape this takes for you, it offers a source of abiding support. Gandhi had a lifelong practice of praying ceaselessly. It started when he was a small boy, when he was scared of almost everything. His nurse suggested that he pray by repeating God's name as a source of comfort and protection. He continued this throughout his whole life as a form of support he offered himself. When he was killed, those who were near heard him praying even as he died.

For many of us, it is an uphill struggle to shift from self-sacrifice to the self-love that nourishes our ability to serve. It's natural to prioritize care for the child nearby, or our loved ones, or to step toward an injustice as it unfolds before us—and we can't help if we've passed out! Exploring my views and struggles around self-love has been generative, and revealing. Perhaps these questions will increase clarity regarding your "care for self" operating instructions:

- What daily practices support you to be your best self?
- Which people in your life love you *and* lovingly challenge you?
- What are the warning signs that you're running on empty?
- What are actions you can do on busy days, or in the middle of a crisis, to stay grounded?

- Can you translate critical self-talk, understanding where those messages come from, and the needs they are trying to meet?
- Can you cultivate habits and practices so that these messages have less and less power?

Your Turn: Stop and appreciate the ways you have learned to care for yourself, even the strategies that may not be as healthy as you would like. These strategies have brought you this far! What daily practices currently nourish you? What are ways you could expand or build ritual for yourself, as well as for and with people you work with?

Heroes: Working for Something Bigger

For fifteen years, I lived near Mt. Hope Cemetery in Rochester, New York, where Susan B. Anthony and Frederick Douglass are buried. As I studied nonviolence and mindfulness, feeling the heartbreak of the world and wondering what I could do, I would visit their graves for inspiration, especially Anthony's. I wanted to learn how to work for something whole-heartedly and enthusiastically without needing it to happen in my lifetime, like she did.

I read letters she wrote toward the end of her life that taught me the value of commitment beyond the scope of my own life. Close, well-meaning friends and family urged her to support partial rights for women so she would have a victory before her death. Anthony refused. Amidst the broad spectrum of strategies and beliefs in the suffragists, Anthony knew she represented the vision of full rights for women; giving up on that position would narrow the national conversation. Equal rights for women were more important than her own validation. Somehow, she recognized—and resisted—the slippery slope of supporting a partial win. Andrew Harvey characterizes this perspective as: "I am here to serve, not to succeed."[46] It is a common thread that runs through all of the people I call heroes.

I saw this attitude in action during a visit to Cape Town, South Africa. I had traveled there with a group led by Arun Gandhi. As we shared tea with Archbishop Desmond Tutu, his daughter Mpho Tutu, and the staff of the Desmond Tutu Foundation, our heads automatically turned toward

---

46. Andrew Harvey, *The Hope: A Guide to Sacred Activism.* I appreciate Andrew Harvey's writing and the explicit connections he makes between spirituality and activism.

Archbishop Tutu. He waved his hands toward his staff and said "Look to them! They are the future." When he said that, we smiled and began to look to one another.

Identifying and studying people we see as heroes deepens understanding of the qualities we wish to embody. In addition to Anthony, King, Tutu, and Gandhi, my heroes include Abdul Ghaffar Khan, Howard Thurman, Vandana Shiva, Fannie Lou Hamer, Nelson Mandela, Eleanor Roosevelt, Dennis Kucinich, and Myles Horton. The list grows. They offer me lessons in courage, perseverance, spiritual depth, sacrifice, vision, and much more. Sharing stories of my heroes, and books about them, is an extension of the pleasure from exploring their lives. A community-building check-in at work could be to ask colleagues to share the identities and stories of their personal heroes.

Each of my heroes' lives were influenced by daily choices and disciplines that, over time, gave rise to their extraordinary legacies. In my search for guidelines for daily living, I use and recommend the following four practices suggested by nonviolence scholar and generous friend Michael Nagler:[47]

- Every day, take time to learn about nonviolence, as a kind of daily vitamin to counteract the idea that violence is inevitable.
- Every day, make time to slow down and know yourself through quiet time, prayer, yoga, or meditation.
- Every day, take some action of any size to make the world better. Listening and service of any kind counts.
- Every day, reduce the consumption of mainstream media, which often makes us fearful and despairing. Make sure the media you consume represents a variety of perspectives, and watch how news from your locality or country is reported in other places.

I invite you to try a 30-day experiment with these practices and notice what changes for you.

Your Turn: Who are your heroes, and why? Can you create opportunities to share the inspiration they offer with others? What support would help you to conduct this 30-day experiment? Would others where you work, worship, or volunteer join you in the experiment, if you asked?

---

47. To learn more from and about Michael Nagler, visit www.mettacenter.org.

Chapter Three Key Ideas

- The gap between stimulus and response offers an opportunity to react in ways that align with our values.
- Contempt dehumanizes self and others and sets the stage for more grievous harm. Uproot contempt by paying attention to where empathy does not flow, by noticing fixed stories, by transforming anger, and by grief work.
- It can be difficult to feel empathy for people we see as holding more power than ourselves. Acknowledging our own power and remembering the humanity of those people can help us to navigate with more skill and more mercy.
- Humans experience internal narratives that influence our outlook. Awareness of the narratives and remembering they are not the whole truth creates space for perspective.
- Get to know your tendencies in response to inevitable pain and suffering. Look for ways to transform suffering that offer fuel for your life.
- Holding grief in groups is an especially powerful strategy for overcoming isolation, and for generating support and insight.
- Anger and fear are intimately connected. Anger is often prompted by care and concern, and knowing this allows us to respond to our own and others' anger with more presence and mercy.
- Reserve anger for systems, rather than directing it toward individuals, as a strategy for systems change.
- Take your own physical, emotional, and spiritual sustenance seriously to sustain the long term efforts required for facing reality and for creating change.
- Identifying those we call heroes, and learning their habits, is a powerful, positive strategy for living with discipline and purpose.

Chapter Four

Nonviolence, in Places We Call Work

Consider your work environment. This may be a home office or a factory, the entertainment business, the medical world, teaching, law enforcement, to name a few. History is witness to the power of the mind of love in action in all of these places and more. Mother Teresa has said that the task is not to do big things but to "do small things with great love." The qualities of generosity, inclusiveness, persistence, spirituality, ethical commitment, and wisdom have stood the test of time.

—Larry Ward & Peggy Rowe Ward

The Importance of Place

The first time I came to the Institute, Kit Miller said, "This is your house now."
She meant that, and I felt it.

—Kristin, served as board member at the M. K. Gandhi Institute

Think of a place—a building, public park, neighborhood, garden, nature—
that makes your whole body feel alive. Feel it? Now consider the opposite:
what happens to your body, mind, and spirit when you walk into a typical
institution, office building, or box store?

Places convey messages and sensations. People can feel welcome and
respected, or invisible and unimportant. Our first impressions of places
inform our early experiences there, providing an opportunity to shift the
culture to one of nonviolence at work.

Both the exterior and interior of the Gandhi Institute were designed to
convey values of inclusion, hospitality, and sustainability. Outside, the
flower and vegetable gardens are varied and beautiful (and almost always
in need of more work). People are welcome to stop by, sit on a bench for a
while, walk the labyrinth, or bring their toddler to the little garden-themed
playground. Murals adorn the warehouse walls behind Gandhi House.
Vegetable beds and fruit trees in the half-acre garden provide produce
to neighbors. Signs welcome people to drop by, in contrast to "private
property, keep off."

Visitors typically enter through the backdoor near the kitchen, a sign of
informality. Inside, they see warm, bright colors on the walls. Artwork is
everywhere. The floors are bamboo hardwood that glow softly on sunlit
days. People are asked to remove their shoes to take care of the floors.
Although this is unusual, especially in workplaces, the Gandhi Institute
sees this as a way of honoring the traditions of people from many parts of
the world for whom this is the respectful way of entering certain spaces. At
many gatherings, food is made onsite in the kitchen and served with dishes
and silverware, not plastic or paper. Guests use handmade cloth napkins.
Sometimes, everyone works together to wash the dishes after the meal. In
the front room, there is a piano where players of all ages and skill levels are
welcomed.

These elements create a liminal space, something between home and public place. This blend is intentional. It causes a creative sense of disorientation. Entering an organizational space that feels like a home tends to pleasantly surprise first time visitors. It helps them relax and sets the stage to find other nontraditional ways in which the Institute works. This energy was intentionally strengthened by the consensual choice for staff to participate in the care and cleaning of the space. The Institute stands out as many spaces used by the public are not well-kept or beautiful. I treasure memories of glad surprise I have seen on faces over the years. My favorite feedback came from a youth who said, "Coming here feels just like going to my grandma's. You ask me to take off my shoes, there's always a snack in the fridge, I can play the piano, and you're glad to see me."

In a world that too often makes people feel unsafe and underappreciated, cultivating places that feel good to humans is a simple, yet profound way to practice nonviolence at work. This attention to space and place contributes significantly to staff well-being too.

When you walk in, you take your shoes off—to respect the house, to respect the people who have been there and built the house. There's an atmosphere of transparency and openness. It's a place where you can be yourself. It's a place where you feel comfortable inviting others, without having to give them a warning about what to expect. It's a place where you can bring your significant other and they will fit right in. It's a place where you can bring your mom or dad, and they're not concerned about where you are working. It's a place that is tough to think about leaving. I can be myself and be understood that I am working on myself. You can ask for help. It's freedom to learn, to be yourself. You don't have to use big words. I often say to people, "It doesn't feel like work." I'm never dreading going to work. By the time you leave that place, you're feeling so rejuvenated. I often wish I'd come here sooner. It's a place to experience loss, grief, happiness, sadness, and you feel that people there are thoroughly excited to see you. Who doesn't want to be in a place like that?
—Natasha, served as staff at the M. K. Gandhi Institute

Your Turn: Look around where you work, worship, and volunteer, and notice aspects that feel depressing, sterile, or even harmful. Talk with colleagues and change what you can. How can your physical spaces signal that people are respected, cared for, and honored?

The Importance of Agreements

Agreements are foundational to all work. They allow us to achieve more together, agreeing on what each person will contribute, how, and when. And yet I find that generally we enter working relationships with silent expectations, making it challenging to get on the same page. Some of the most important modeling and trust-building any of us can do relates to agreements: making them, keeping them, ending them with care and consciousness when they no longer serve.

Cocreating group norms and agreements offers an opportunity to reflect on the means the group wants to employ to reach its ends. How do members want to be treated, and to treat others? What conditions will inspire trust and courage? A best practice in norms is to review them each time the group meets as a reminder and a chance to refresh and recommit, and keep them visible. Norms and agreements foster group accountability.[48]

While the particular agreements change from group to group, here's an example of how one group honors agreements. (More on group agreements follows in chapter 6.) In my work with them, I have been fortunate to see how the Indigenous Peoples Committee in Rochester takes its agreements, called group commitments, seriously. Any meeting is an opportunity to change and update these. Everyone reads them together. We pause and consider them each time.

- Be in a good mind.
- Be conscious of language.
- Prioritize the voices of Indigenous People.
- Embrace discomfort.
- Assume good intentions, monitor impact.
- Listen for understanding.
- Be open.
- Be respectful of culture.
- Show willingness to learn.
- Be curious.
- Learn about historical and current issues relative to Indigenous People.
- Be comfortable with unfinished conversations.
- Take space, make space.

---

48. Check out page 175 for staff commitments and feedback process collaboratively developed at the Gandhi Institute.

- Be aware of blanket statements.
- Be aware of "colonizer mind" behaviors. (See article "White Supremacy Culture."[49] Commit to reading the article, be aware of behaviors, and call them when we see them.)
- While sharing stories with others outside our group for the purpose of learning, keep confidential any identifying information of the storyteller.
- Check in to see if people all know each other before starting the meeting.
- Celebrate successes.
- Be intentional about building relationships among group members in and outside of our monthly meeting.
- Think with your heart and not your head.
- Have fun and enjoy the journey.

When entering a new agreement or making a decision, the more important an agreement or decision, the slower I go. This can feel counterintuitive to some people since big decisions often come with big pressure. Few decisions are so urgent and unexpected that it is not possible to take time to marinate. Try to give people time to check with themselves and back out. Whenever possible, let people sleep on promises or commitments. This balances the pressure or inspiration of the moment with a deeper sense of reflection. We often say we will do things, only to later realize it was unrealistic, unwise, or unmanageable to see it through.

During the large fundraisers (500+ people) we organized for Bay Area Nonviolent Communication, I would call people who made large gifts within a day. This was to thank them, of course, *and* to offer an explicit opportunity to change their mind. Giving this space to people meant that our agreements were solid. (The calls were much appreciated, we received useful feedback for future fundraising, and—amazingly—no gift was reduced.)

All agreements have expiration dates . . . every one, even the most cherished. This is important to acknowledge. Because of our varied relationships to transition, it can be hard for people to move on. Some of us rush changes or endings (me!) and others avoid them until the bitter end.[50]

---

49. See chapter 5 for a discussion on white supremacy culture.
50. William Bridges's book *Transitions: Making Sense of Life's Changes* is one I recommend when a change is looming.

The notion that agreements expire covers everything from what to have for dinner to how we govern ourselves. Think about the US Constitution: its original agreement excluded 96 percent of the populace. The arc of this nation's social justice struggles has reshaped that document many times over. Yet, these versions of our political agreements expire too. The Chilean people have updated their constitution several times—and were doing so again as I wrote sections of this book—after mass protests against the limitations of the dictatorship-era constitution. Goals for the proposed new constitution include envisioning a stronger government role in providing social services, advancing gender parity, and protecting indigenous groups and the environment.[51] Pretty inspiring!

Denial that agreements change can create extra difficulties when ending working relationships. Many of us have seen tension, hurt feelings, and secret plotting to make an exit. We can make it easier for people to conclude their time by signaling care through ongoing conversation regarding goals and future plans from day one. When that inevitable moment comes—hopefully years later, whether they're going to another job, moving, or turning to educational pursuits—a nonviolent approach is to acknowledge the transition, and to engage them with helping to pass their knowledge on in whatever ways make sense. The end of a work relationship doesn't need to be fraught with secrecy, or discomfort. It can be anchored in gratitude and openness and celebration.

Ends, conclusions, and releases are part of the cycle of living systems. This is true not just for employment, but also for projects and tasks. Periodically, either annually or on some other rhythm, check in with colleagues about their roles and responsibilities to explore what needs to be let go or tweaked. These conversations are not performance evaluations; they are opportunities to change tactics to maximize vitality, ongoing learning, and our unique gifts. Start with what has worked well, what has been meaningful or even beautiful. From there, move to challenges. Sometimes, you will find a person has been grappling with upheaval at home, health issues, pursuing graduate education, or is interested in doing different kinds of work. This can present the chance to open the conversation to cover the person's long term plans, which may include wrapping up their time with you, and how to facilitate a thoughtful process for bringing in new people. When I was conducting these conversations at the Institute, they often occurred in the spring as part of our planning and budget process

---

51. https://www.americasquarterly.org/article/chiles-proposed-constitution-7-key-points/

for the next fiscal year (July 1–June 30). The synergy between the wishes of team members and the forecasted needs of the organization to pursue and achieve strategic goals became a reliable, participatory method to set a viable framework for the coming year.

Sometimes we offer to help with something and realize afterward that it was not a great idea. Maybe our partner reminds us of an earlier commitment. Perhaps we recall the ten other things on our plate that week, or our schedule unexpectedly shifts. Whatever the reason, it's not uncommon for human beings to have to back out of an offer. I frequently find that people's hearts are bigger than their calendars.

If you notice a volunteer or a colleague who isn't showing up, making excuses, or juggling a lot, it might help them to think about and perhaps release a commitment. When you see someone not being as present as they were, or who is not meeting deadlines, approach them as quickly as you can to check on them.

To embody nonviolence during this conversation, remember to seek to understand, rather than to be understood. Finding this clarity is not easy. Feelings of frustration, hurt, or resentment can fester when someone is dropping balls or flaking on you. It can help to talk things over with a third person ahead of time so you can be present and clear with the individual struggling to meet their commitments.

Look for a non-pressured moment to check in, and ask if they need to be "blessed and released." Be ready to listen. People frequently feel defensive, unhappy, or guilty when they can't do what they promised. Listening to concerns or regret frees them to offer another way to contribute. And if that doesn't happen, you still keep a friend (or committed supporter). Keep an eye on the long run in all your relations.

Your turn: When you reflect on agreements that you have not been able to keep, what learning is there? Are there patterns such as timing, or difficulties asking support? How can that awareness help you consciously make and keep agreements with others?

Honor Humanness

The Institute is creating an alternative in how we work, an alternative to "rise and grind."
—Matt, served as staff at the M. K. Gandhi Institute

The people we work with are human beings. Humans love, mourn, exalt, despair, get sick, heal, care for families and friends, yearn for adventure, delight in ceremony and celebration, enjoy music and art, wrestle with doubt, grow bored, get passionate, and embody a thousand more nuances of existence. It is a form of nonviolence to cultivate spaces that honor and respect everyone. Places where we work, worship, and volunteer can embrace the messy, beautiful complexity of being human.

Many organizations—including faith communities, schools, and nonprofits—expect people to show up day after day, without much acknowledgement of the natural ebb and flow of creativity, focus, and enthusiasm. Significant experiences in people's lives may be under-respected, sometimes acknowledged only because of laws, as with parental and sick leave policies. Realities of childcare and eldercare are often left unaccounted, as are disabilities in the employee or in their family. Different learning styles and modes of expression are infrequently understood or accommodated, and rarely celebrated. These acts of alienation, small and large, undermine our spirits and undermine the potential each day offers for meaning and contribution.

The COVID-19 pandemic demonstrated that the typical structure of work—which seemed set in stone for decades—can, indeed, be changed, and rapidly. These adaptations are reminders that we can experiment and transform work to be more respectful, nourishing, and compassionate. Honoring individual and collective humanity in as many ways as possible offers a compass for navigating future challenges. It can also build something called Beloved Community.

Beloved Community is a term made popular by Dr. Martin Luther King Jr. and coined by Josiah Royce in 1913. For me, the term has come to mean a vision of a world or society or even a circle of coworkers where everyone knows they matter and are valued. There is a sense of dynamic belonging which does not exclude conflict, divergence, and difference.

Here are a few ideas to try that honor everyone's humanness:

Regular check-ins: Ongoing check-ins give people opportunities to share joys and sorrows, or their "rose and thorn" that day. Sometimes, it can reveal why someone is showing up differently than usual, and offers colleagues ongoing opportunities to exchange support. Check-ins are foundational practices in community building in groups.

Learning and expression styles: We can incorporate many modes of expression into our work, including art, videos, oral communications, podcasts, storytelling, theater and role plays, charts and graphs, numbers and data, music, even movement. Find out how your colleagues love to express their ideas. Play to their strengths. Incorporate their passions. Make a habit of asking: What other formats could we use?

Growth edges and learning curves: Each of us seeks chances to learn and practice new skills and understandings. A nonviolent approach to celebrating humanness is to find space for each individual to explore their growth edges. At the same time, as we learn new skills, we make mistakes. When building in space for learning, remember to allow for learning curves. Most challenges, whether creating a new product or working to reduce a social ill, are complex and cannot be resolved easily. Those who work on them require support, resilience, and encouragement to "fail faster."

Shifting roles and responsibilities: Wherever possible, rotate tasks and roles to encourage colleagues to experience the full range of their humanness—confidence, confusion, uncertainty, and proficiency alike.

Changing horizons: As mentioned in the section on agreements, check in with people regularly about their roles. What remains life-giving in their current set of responsibilities? What is on their horizon that they can use help with? Are they considering marriage, retirement, grad school, or some other move? What needs to change to incorporate that horizon into their life at work?

Four-day work week: This schedule is designed to allow time for personal pursuits, doctor's appointments, long weekends, and other needs. It has been shown to increase—not decrease—productivity.

Vacations: Having *paid* vacations is a form of equity that ensures everyone, regardless of finances, feels able to use their vacation time. In addition to a generous vacation policy, it can be useful to make sure staff understand that they can take time off to observe their faith traditions, including personal retreats, or non-institutional expressions of spiritual practice. Many may need encouragement to actually use this benefit—our culture ingrains workaholism into us from a young age.

Health care and sick leave: A deeply tangible expression of care for people is providing support for physical and mental health. Groups and organizations can express this care through ongoing conversations and cocreated policies with members regarding their needs, and enacting the most creative and generous policies possible. Since people's needs differ, these conversations are a generative space for leaning into Beloved Community. Cocreating clearly-articulated policies offers even more support to those who struggle to take good care of their health.

Parental leave: Having a child is a momentous experience—one of the top ten most significant things that can happen in a human lifetime. Honoring this by offering parental leave for parents of all genders is a form of nonviolence. Whether they are adopting, giving birth, or the partner of a pregnant person, offer generous support to truly sink into this experience. When parental leave ends, consider how else your organization can embrace the joys and challenges of parenthood. For example, sleep deprivation is normal for first-year parents. Can your team keep track of deadlines and details in a caring way, knowing that the parent on staff might be less alert than usual?

Childcare and eldercare: Many human beings are caring for other human beings, notably children and elders. This comes with inconvenient schedules in our world, as children go to daycare, school, babysitters, or after-school programs; and elders need to be brought to doctor's appointments or assisted in other ways. Consider hosting a one-time or ongoing gathering with those colleagues to appreciate their extra effort to manage work/life balance. Ask them to share strategies and ideas on how they juggle these commitments and how their workplace can more consciously support them.

Mourning, grief, depression: In addition to time off for funerals, there are ways our organizations can be gentle with people moving through grief. After losing a loved one, or a devastating community or world event, people experience sorrow, exhaustion, lack of focus, and more. Human beings do not have an on/off switch for grief, nor for its close cousins, despair and depression. What aspects of each person's role are non-negotiable and must be completed, regardless of grief, and which can be reassigned or set aside for a while? Discuss this with them—each person experiences grief differently.

The communal aspect of working at the Institute is so special—it's like the inside of a watch, everything connected and running. All these things are happening and we're still able to make people feel seen and heard. I just love when we're all together putting on an event.
—Chyna, served as staff at the M. K. Gandhi Institute

Your turn: When have you been met with humanity from work and volunteer commitments during a big life event? How did it feel to be cared about in that way? List a few new ways people can receive and exchange support. Think of 2–3 that could be implemented right away, and 2–3 that might require planning and additional budget. Be fearless with your ideas!

About Money

I challenge you to move the resources that flow through your life toward your highest commitments and ideals, those things you stand for. I challenge you to hold money as a common trust that we're all responsible for using in ways that nurture and empower us, and all life, our planet, and all future generations.
—Lynne Twist

In applying the concept of nonviolence at work, decisions regarding money are a tangible place where "the rubber meets the road." With colleagues, I've experimented with how money comes into the workplace, what we do with it while we have it, and where (and how) it goes out.

For sixteen years, I was privileged to work at nonprofit organizations that operated from the policy that no individual or group would be turned away for lack of funds. This approach was built on ease of access, replacing protracted scholarship processes with quick, respectful conversations. Mutuality, trust, and exchange are emphasized to reduce the risk of the mutually-disempowering "handout" mentality. Sometimes individuals end up contributing as volunteers; other times people prefer to offer cash at a later date when they have funds available again. Sometimes people just take the gift and that's fine. We are achieving our mission if they are with us, engaging and learning.

This approach meant that our events often included more diverse populations, including young people, people who are not employed, and retired folk. Finding ways to remove economic barriers for participation makes good sense. Including people with varied financial resources made events a better value for everyone, offering opportunities for people of different classes and ages to genuinely connect.

For many, unemployment offers an ironic twist of fate: just when we have more time for learning, we have fewer resources to pay. Since our mission included public education, when I heard that someone had lost their job, I often invited them to take every opportunity to participate, and give back only when it felt doable. Depending on the mission of your workplace, this might look different. When unemployment impacts someone's sense of worth or life direction, receiving support, learning, and community become even more vital, and potentially transformative.

Another place to practice nonviolence in relation to money is pay structures. Regarding compensation, stop and think: What range of remuneration feels fair? What would you like the least paid person in an organization, whether for-profit or non-profit, to make? What about remuneration for those at the top?

This question helps clarify values and "put our money where our mouth is." Pay inequality has become enormous especially in large corporations, with some hourly workers making an annual salary that their CEOs receive in just one hour.[52] At the Gandhi Institute, the ratio between the highest-paid person (me) and the least-paid was 2½:1. Our commitment to that pay range ensured that everyone did better together.[53]

Because of its practical and symbolic importance, where money is stored and how it is used matters. Local credit unions and banks often have

---

52. https://www.theguardian.com/us-news/2022/jun/07/us-wage-gap-ceos-workers-institute-for-policy-studies-report
53. To deepen your understanding of the truly remarkable consequences that increased economic equality has on social systems, I recommend the book *The Spirit Level: Why Greater Equality Makes Societies Stronger* by Kate Pickett and Richard Wilkinson.

policies that align with principles of nonviolence in terms of local lending policies, supporting local service groups, and consciousness regarding not funding industries responsible for environmental harm or militarism. (This varies, so do your research.) In addition to banking locally, consider concentrating purchasing with local companies and businesses owned by People of the Global Majority.

Each place where you are a stakeholder—as a student, employee, bank customer, retirement account holder, investor, etc.—provides an opportunity to put your values into action. It's exciting to learn about ways that this has been done to support socially-just policy changes in institutions, such as activism on college campuses and with teachers unions to direct endowments and pension funds toward socially responsive investment. [54]

Your Turn: How are decisions about money made where you work, worship, or volunteer? What spaces exist to ask questions about how resources are allocated and about the values those decisions reflect? How can transparency and accountability on these topics be increased?

Cultural Humility

Culture is a reflection of what you value. . . . What existed in the culture of the Institute was dedication to looking at what was real.
—Kristin, served as board member at the M. K. Gandhi Institute

In 1998, Melanie Tervalon and Jann Murray-Garcia were working as a physician and nurse practitioner at Oakland Children's Hospital in Oakland, California. Because of the enormously diverse population the hospital served, they recognized the need for a process to support staff in navigating cultural needs of patients and each other. **Cultural humility** is a process and a mindset for learning, perspective, and behavior change in relation to cultural identity.

The same need exists in other spaces. No amount of training on the details of each culture (cultural competency) can adequately prepare us for the breadth of diversity we will encounter. Think about who might walk through the doors where you work, worship, or volunteer—neurodivergent people;

---

54. Morgan Simon's book *Real Impact: The New Economics of Social Change* inspired me on this topic.

deaf individuals using sign language; refugees struggling with culture shock and often trauma; LGBTQIA couples; Black, Brown, and Indigenous families . . . the list is endless. In practice, like Tervalon and Murray-Garcia, every organization needs an *approach* that can guide respectful interactions with everyone.

I'd like to draw your attention to two important aspects of how cultural humility structures respect. The first is that it shifts the concept of cultural understanding away from static thinking, i.e. *I already know about racism, or sexism, or bias toward others, because I took a class;* or *I have a friend who is (fill in the blank)*. Cultural humility calls instead for a process orientation. Regardless of our identity, education, and experience, we acknowledge that we are inevitably less-informed about other people's culture, experiences, and challenges than they are. Remembering this changes our internal default setting from "I should already know this" to "it's okay to not know." This shifts guilt and denial toward a wonderfully relieving humility. With respect, we can inquire about what we don't know.

The second aspect is that this framework is useful to all, regardless of the identities within your group, and therefore unifying. Everyone benefits from learning cultural humility, from a task force on poverty to a faith community to a neighborhood park planning committee. Through an ongoing focus on cultural humility, we remember that respect literally means "to look, again." Leaders benefit by remembering that every person in an organization has something to teach them. Clients and customers benefit from the built-in respect that cultural humility engenders in those who seek to practice it.

In 2016, cultural humility was embraced by the Gandhi Institute's diverse team. We operationalized it by weaving it into our staff commitments and later into staff feedback processes. Claiming cultural humility as an organizational value (and embedding it in our practices and policies) offered clarity in how to create an increasingly human-centered way to relate.

Your Turn: How might cultural humility support an effort you are involved with? Does it relieve any pressure to imagine yourself utilizing this way of knowing, being, and doing?

Embodying Cultural Humility

We all must deal with conditioning. The sense of ourselves as separate is what we are contending with virtually all of the time. It's our curriculum, and everybody's enrolled.

—Ram Dass

Cultural humility is both a framework and a practice for knowing, being, and doing. As with the other ideas in this text, seeing through this new framework is only the first step. The efforts that follow to apply the concepts to situations in your life are where the real magic happens. Here are some examples of how to embody the three tenets of cultural humility.

Tenet 1: Critical Self-Reflection and Lifelong Learning

Is there something you love learning about? Perhaps music, gardening, cooking, or a new language? When we feel excited or passionate about a subject, it's joyful to acknowledge that there is always more to learn. The first tenet of cultural humility asks us to bring that same enthusiasm to understanding the astonishing diversity among human beings. It's a topic for potentially endless study of race and gender, and also class, faith, worldview, disability, sexual orientation, profession, talents, challenges, citizenship, family history, and so much more. Continuous learning and critical self-reflection helps us to relax with not knowing, and sets the table for authentic interactions and questions. Members of the Gandhi Institute have said that the orientation of cultural humility as lifelong learning encouraged commitment, trust, and facilitated meaningful team building.

At the Gandhi Institute, one way we embodied this tenet was through holding collective learning opportunities. Sometimes this was offered by an outside person and sometimes we learned from within our team. My favorite example of this comes from my colleague Erin Thompson who kept a running list of frequently-used language, such as anti-racism, privilege, restorative justice, and nonviolence. As a group, we would periodically choose 2–3 words from the list. Each of us would write our definition and share them in pairs, then with our team (usually 10–12 people). The goal was not to find a shared definition, but to listen deeply and critically self-reflect on the ways our understandings overlapped *and* diverged. I invite you to try this activity with a group. You might be surprised, or maybe not, with the differing understanding people bring to commonly used words.

I like that staff don't have to agree on everything in order to do really good work. There's some fundamental disagreements, and that's okay. It's refreshing, there's no fake kumbaya. They genuinely care about the work and each other and they don't have to agree.

—Jessica, served as board member at the M. K. Gandhi Institute

Tenet 2: Challenge Power Imbalances

Challenging power imbalances connects to several other themes in this book: awareness of rank (page 135), building and maintaining trust (page 132), and continuous feedback (page 154). These practices help to reveal and foster communication about issues of power and power imbalances.

Many or even most people I work with report feeling conflict-averse, so speaking up when a power imbalance is occurring is not easy. Since challenging power can feel so, well, challenging, here are several strategies.

One is the framework of *intention and impact* as a method to communicate concerns. Most of us are not aware of our power, and do not intend to abuse it.[55] The framework of intention and impact helps acknowledge benign intentions while addressing harmful impact. This can help us overcome the tendency to defend our actions by focusing on intent, which dismisses the experience of the other. Holding both truths can be especially helpful in a conflict or dilemma that involves a power dynamic. It can help the person with more power to hear and absorb the impact on the other and to deprioritize the focus on intention, to build trust and offer more opportunities to learn.

A second strategy is the Nonviolent Communication (NVC) framework. In it, we state an observation about the imbalance, name our universal needs (and related feelings, if the environment feels right to do so), and seek strategies to meet those needs. A framework like Nonviolent Communication can boost skill, courage, and confidence. One example occurred

---

55. One reason that people are unaware of impact is a lack of understanding about power. I recommend Cyndi Suarez's book *The Power Manual: How to Master Complex Power Dynamics* and the work of Amy and Arnold Mindell on rank and privilege.

during a feedback session with a staff member who expressed frustration that I was the only team member who had not moved to the Google platform. Although I had been nudged in that direction by others, her frank observation helped me to see that my choice not only was inconvenient for others, it reflected power dynamics on our team. Because I was the senior staff member, I could "get away" with not shifting. I also realized that I felt overwhelmed about tech and the time involved in learning a new system. Stating this unlocked our shared power to make change. She offered to help me learn my way around the new platform and we agreed on a time frame for the transition, which helped both of us.

The third strategy to challenge power imbalances is borrowed from restorative practices and includes mindsets and questions that shift focus from assigning blame to care for all parties: What happened? How have you and others been affected? What could we decide to do together to address what happened and if possible, make it right? These questions, and questions like them, help empower the person with less power in a situation to be active in creating resolution.

Tenet 3: Institutional Accountability

Institutions change slowly. One barrier to change can be a lack of trust that any new commitment will be sustained. For instance, the commitment that many organizations made to anti-racism after the murder of George Floyd appears to be fading.[56] Unless they are moved into policy and procedure, even the most excellent innovations fade when circumstances and personnel change. In several organizations, I have supported anti-racism change teams composed of individuals from diverse, multi-racial, multi-disciplinary backgrounds. These teams involved hundreds of people in different fields. One workplace was unionized, others were not. From the beginning, these teams spent significant time building relationships and articulating shared agreements. They learned ways to engage in difficult conversations, as well as identifying steps their group could take to move forward with anti-racism work. Throughout, my colleagues and I recommended a focus on being (relationship building and learning together) as well as doing. This groundwork set the foundation for these groups to sustain their efforts over time.

---

56. https://www.wsj.com/business/fewer-black-professionals-are-getting-promoted-into-management-reversing-trend-e2e002d5

Tenets in action

The three tenets of cultural humility create a reinforcing loop[57] within groups and institutions. On a personal level, the tenets of cultural humility clarify my values and focus my attention. Recently, I did not make a change to a document that my colleague and I were preparing for an event, and sent it to our clients anyway. After we discussed it, I apologized. I saw that I had been caught up in urgency twice—first not taking time to understand the tweak she was suggesting, and second choosing to send the document without checking with her. Critical self-reflection (tenet 1) rescued our connection and helped me especially to harvest the learning.

Interrupting power imbalances (tenet 2) has been a similarly powerful practice. For instance, a few years ago, I joined forty people at a diversity and inclusion committee meeting during its annual meeting with the institutional leader. During the hour-long meeting, I noted that for the first thirty minutes only white people spoke. So when it came to my turn, I said, "I notice that we've only heard from white folks in the room and so instead of making my point, I'd like to ask that we open the space to hear from Brown and Black colleagues."

I had forgotten the incident until, years later, a white doctor did the same thing. Afterward, she told me she had learned to do it from hearing me in that other meeting. That was great feedback and a reminder of how much our choices matter. Even if people don't mention it at the time, they pick up on our behaviors. My default setting is to always act like someone is watching.

At the Gandhi Institute, we increased our accountability (tenet 3) through a feedback structure that was created by several team members, and approved by all. We utilized group interviews when onboarding new staff and board members. When hiring new staff, or speaking to potential board members, we asked the same set of questions: to speak about their racial identity journey thus far, and about their interest in ongoing, often challenging conversations about equity and anti-racism. These questions deepened conversations and conveyed values.

Understanding more about each, we can start to see the flow of how all three tenets of cultural humility work together. As we approach learning with eager openness, we recognize ways to challenge power imbalances

---

57. https://www.systems-thinking.org/theWay/sre/re.htm

in ourselves and others. This helps us see how institutions can be more accountable in implementing policy and practices that break down those imbalances—or prevent them from arising. Institutional accountability encourages individuals to engage in self-reflection and lifelong learning, making more space for understanding different cultures.

Your Turn: How might your work benefit from consistently employing the three tenets of cultural humility? Is there another approach that you have learned to support continuous learning and action to heal from our collective harmful conditioning?

Chapter Four Key Ideas

- Agreements are foundational to every kind of work and relationship. Be mindful regarding the conscious creation and ongoing need to refresh agreements.
- Honor humanness—the ebb and flow of creativity, focus, and enthusiasm that go with the various demands and experiences in our lives.
- Places convey messages, and set the tone for what happens within.
- How money flows into and out of the workplace offers abundant opportunities to put nonviolence principles into practice.
- Cultural humility is a framework and practice that calls on us to remember and act from understanding that we are inevitably less-informed about others' culture, experiences, and challenges than they are.
- The three tenets of cultural humility—critical self-reflection and lifelong learning, challenging power imbalances, and institutional accountability—create a reinforcing loop to help create a human-centered way to be and work together.

Chapter Five
Value Shifts

We were located in a Black neighborhood, working in schools with Black and Brown children. That's why, during my time on the board, we had to embody racial justice, not just talk about social justice.

—Kristin, served as board member at the M. K. Gandhi Institute

Human salvation lies in the hands of the creatively maladjusted.

—Dr. Martin Luther King Jr.

In *The Politics of Communication*, author Claus Mueller asserts that "one of the functions of ideologies is the legitimation of domination."[58] Dominant cultural values in the United States are not neutral, and these include values that shape norms and behaviors where we work, worship, and volunteer—attitudes regarding punctuality, overwork, biases in hiring, expectations regarding appearance, social cliques that predetermine promotions, how conflicts are handled, and more. Standards of "professionalism" arose under the values of white supremacy.

White supremacy is a loaded phrase. Depending on your age and identity, it may bring up images of burning crosses and intentional acts of violence, cruelty, and exclusion, or it may represent the hundreds of thousands of interactions, large and small, where bias is occurring. Because all of us are exposed to these values from birth, we bear the consequences of having our thinking and behavior shaped through these values, regardless of our race. *This conditioning happened without our consent and almost entirely outside our conscious awareness.* Understanding and changing these "deep structures"— the assumptions, values, and incentives that determine our most basic decision-making processes—has been shown to be key to lasting change.[59] We will talk more about these structures in chapter 9.

In *White Supremacy Culture: Still Here,* Tema Okun and colleagues describe the characteristics of white supremacy culture as "ideas and attitudes that perpetuate internalized racial superiority through white supremacy and impact Black, Indigenous, and people of color in ways that increase internalized inferiority." In addition to the fear that is created via these norms and behaviors within people of all races, Okun names fifteen other characteristics of white supremacy:

A SENSE OF URGENCY	PROGRESS IS BIGGER, MORE	POWER HOARDING
WORSHIP OF THE WRITTEN WORD	QUANTITY OVER QUALITY	FEAR OF OPEN CONFLICT
PERFECTIONISM	INDIVIDUALISM	OBJECTIVITY
DEFENSIVENESS	ONLY ONE "RIGHT WAY"	"I'M THE ONLY ONE"
PATERNALISM	EITHER/OR THINKING	RIGHT TO COMFORT

58. Claus Mueller, *The Politics of Communication: A Study in the Political Sociology of Language, Socialization, and Legitimation*, 108.
59. Connie Gersick, "Revolutionary Change Theories: A Multilevel Exploration of the Punctuated Equilibrium Paradigm," *The Academy of Management Review* 16, No. 1 (January 1991): 10-36.

The identifiable characteristics of white supremacy culture are revealing. In organizations, the costs of white supremacy include loss of talent, trust, and creativity, as well as increased stress, turnover, legal expenses and more. In society, the consequences of white supremacy hurt people everywhere. For example, 80 percent of the mass shootings in the US in 2022 are estimated to be influenced by white supremacy.[60]

Violence comes in myriad forms. Learning to see the characteristics of white supremacy can help us identify and uproot patterns of power such as "my way or the highway" and patterns of thinking that limit possibilities, like the notion that creating win-win solutions is a luxury rather than necessity.[61] Reading these characteristics, can you imagine some of the problems and the harm that arise from these deep structures of thought and behavior?

Fortunately, Tema Okun and colleagues also offer antidotes to white supremacy culture, which point the way toward building a culture of nonviolence at work and elsewhere. They recommend focusing attention on the antidotes, rather than using the characteristics as a new way to judge behavior. For example, I referred to them to ensure that the material in this book—and the process of writing it—aligned with those recommendations.

The following sections of this chapter highlight specific strategies for ways of working that embody some of these antidotes: relation to time, rethinking the idea of mistakes, and valuing the perspectives of all.

Your Turn: Do you recognize any characteristics of white supremacy as challenges for you? Do you see them as a characteristic of people you know, or of the culture in workplaces where you spend time? What do you think may be some consequences of these cultural norms?

It's About Time

What still impacts me today (ten years later) is taking time to connect and understand with people—basically, slowing down to go faster.

—Thomas, served as board member at the M. K. Gandhi Institute

---

60. https://www.reuters.com/world/us/white-supremacists-behind-over-80-extremism-related-us-murders-2022-2023-02-23/
61. Listen to economist Heather McGhee to learn how racism hurts everyone in these United States: https://www.ted.com/talks/heather_c_mcghee_racism_has_a_cost_for_everyone.

At board meetings, check-in times can go way beyond the agenda. And that is the backbone of our time together—not only sharing how we're feeling but also having the opportunity to have it reflected back to us. Sometimes we need to spend more time, and that always comes first. That's one of the reasons why people who go to Gandhi Institute board meetings can leave feeling super energized, again and again.

—Joel, served as board member at the M. K. Gandhi Institute

Time is a fluid concept. In the introduction to his 1982 book, *The Dance of Life*, anthropologist Edward T. Hall points out that time is a core framework of cultural, social, and personal life. Humans think about and experience time differently from one another. The Anishinaabe see time as flowing in all directions like ripples on a lake, as Robin Wall Kimmerer writes in *Braiding Sweetgrass*. Many European cultures think of time as a line. From my experience, attitudes about time within the United States vary somewhat by region. People with more wealth are reported to experience time differently compared to those with less wealth.[62]

These diverse cultural norms about time are usually unspoken and frequently collide. In groups, relationships to time are often markers for respect, or lack thereof. In mainstream US culture, being prompt shows respect. These attitudes derive in part from the sense of urgency and other characteristics named on page 78. Those who arrive after an event or meeting has begun may be viewed as unreliable, or disrespectful.

Many groups operate from the sense that time is scarce. At meetings or in speaking, people rush to cram in as much as possible. Some feel self-conscious about "taking up the group's time," so their contributions or useful objections go unheard. People who seem not to have that inter-nalized understanding may be judged as disruptive or selfish, unless they have higher rank or status within the group.

In short, tensions can arise from unexamined, habitual assumptions. These assumptions are left unspoken and are—especially in multi-cultural, multi-generational groups—not universal, which sometimes results in resentment and misunderstandings. I find consciousness of these dynamics to be highly valuable. When scarcity of time causes friction, ask the group to pause and pay attention to their values around process vs. outcome. This is especially

---

62. https://www.nationalgeographic.com/science/article/how-you-perceive-time-may-depend-on-income-memory-formation

revealing in low-trust settings where individuals are withholding their honest perspectives. When urgency seems to routinely rule the space, it's a useful time to draw attention to the process. Often a collective sigh of relief ensues, trust begins to rise, and creativity kicks in. Often, not always!

By exploring beliefs about time, especially when tensions exist about it, we can see the variations in how each of us measure it and treasure it. This offers an opportunity to try on new viewpoints and to recognize that conceptions about time are shaped by cultural norms. While there is no right or wrong relationship to time, consciousness of our diverse approaches offers clarity and power to make aware choices. We can dismantle habitual "default" settings (punctuality, time scarcity, strict agendas) and notice that centering relationships, rather than time management, creates a different quality to gatherings. Benefits include more authentic interactions, accelerated decision making, and increased willingness to take risks and make mistakes.

Your Turn: Notice your habits relating to time. What patterns do you see in your thinking and behavior, and in the way you view others? What judgments have tended to arise in the past? Consider exploring attitudes about time as part of check-ins and retreats.

Mistakes: Opportunities for Learning and Connection

My mom says that expectations are premeditated resentments.
—Student at the University of Rochester

As a staff member, everything I was taught to believe, the mental models I was given, are being challenged: ideas about what success means, what community means, or what health means, even. All of that is being challenged. We don't have it all figured out—we're trying to figure it out together.
—Bianca, served as staff at the M. K. Gandhi Institute

The inner harshness that many of us carry—a result of conditioning and cultural messages—is at its most fierce when we err. This is likely a consequence of two characteristics of white supremacy culture named by Okun and colleagues: "perfectionism" and "only one right way." Fear of screwing up can, among other things, keep us playing small with our lives.

What we call mistakes are as inevitable as gravity and in most settings, little cause for alarm. When the error is yours, get support in working through its emotional impact on you—whether that be fear or mourning or shame—and then move as swiftly as possible to make amends.

Jazz pianist Frank Barrett speaks about the perspective jazz offers on the willingness to risk mistakes to build something greater. He says jazz musicians, in a sense, engage in "constructive arguments."[63] Fear of making mistakes, however, limits the beautiful complexity of the music as people try to keep things simple.

We can create spaces within and between ourselves to reduce this anxiety, including in high pressure situations. Jazz musicians like Miles Davis were wary of work that essentially repeated itself. Davis evidently forbade musicians who played with him to practice, to avoid developing comfortable musical motifs that they would later rely upon during performances. Instead, he challenged them to perform at the edges of their abilities and creativity.

Trusting people enough to let them fail is one of my favorite ways to inspire confidence in others. At the Gandhi Institute, we did this by changing individual responsibilities regularly, creating different teams to work on projects and events, and by adding new pieces and approaches to our work. Frequent use of feedback (explored more on page 154) normalized opportunities for learning. A mistake or missed opportunity was welcomed, not punished. For new staff, volunteers, interns, and board members, seeing this conveyed our lived values more powerfully than any written statement or handbook could. During interviews for this book, relaxing with mistakes was one of the practices named as most supportive of healing, learning, and commitment.

Myles Horton, founder of the Highlander Folk School where people like Rosa Parks, Septima Clark, and Dr. King spent time, tells a story about trusting people enough to let them fail even in tense circumstances. Horton speaks of a gathering of union leaders in a hotel room in rural North Carolina in the 1930s. The union was on strike and the strike wasn't going well. They were starting to run low on money, the governor was going to call in the National Guard, and they were getting desperate to know what their next move would be. So, they were kind of ripping their hair out.

---

63. Frank J. Barrett, *Yes to the Mess: Surprising Leadership Lessons from Jazz*, 110.

Horton says he was in the room quietly observing and a man turned to him and said, "Well, hell! You're the experienced person here, tell us what to do!" And Horton says that he thought to himself, "If I tell them what to do now, how will they know what to do next time without me? And how will they build trust in themselves that they don't need me?" Even if they made a mistake, that process was more valuable to Horton than allowing them to defer to him. And so he said to the guy, "I'm sorry, I can't tell you what to do." Even after the man pulled out a gun and said, "If you don't tell me what to do, I'm going to kill you!" he held his ground.[64]

I love that story because it illustrates how desperately we sometimes want people to take responsibility for us. For me, part of being a leader that's self-connected is also being willing to just let people fall down sometimes and let them figure it out for themselves. It's all a balance.

When an effort doesn't work in the way you wanted it to, talk it over and harvest the learning. Sometimes, the hard-won lessons are the real payoff. These kernels of wisdom often circle around and lead to success in another iteration. It is powerful when colleagues show others that they dare to shake things up and move outside their comfort zone.[65]

Your Turn: How do you relate to yourself when you mess up? Is there a connection to what you were taught as a child about mistakes? What can you offer yourself, and others, to help relax with mistakes?

Reducing "Shoulds," Increasing Authentic Effort

The Institute is a very nurturing space, with a lot of respect for autonomy. It's okay to say I'm not at my best right now and know there will be no judgment. I'm not sure why people everywhere don't understand that if you treat people well, they will work their hardest for you.

—Chyna, served as staff at the M. K. Gandhi Institute

Don't should on me, and I won't should on you.

—David Roth

---

64. Like Anne Braden, who also dedicated her life to confronting racism during that era, Horton was a white southerner. Their autobiographies, included in resources at the end of this book, are worth reading.
65. *Creative Confidence: Unleashing the Creative Potential Within Us All* by Tom and David Kelley is a useful read on cultivating courage and innovation.

What inspires motivation in you? What about people you work with? In places where you work or serve, is it common for people to have authentic enthusiasm for the mission? With staff and volunteers, work to reduce "should" thinking. "Should" thinking shows up as a murky combination of fear, anxiety, and the habitual energy of being without choice. Honoring autonomy and reducing "should" thinking is another way to embody antidotes to perfectionism, defensiveness, and either/or thinking.

Generally, I prefer tasks not to be done rather than be completed under duress or with a preponderance of "should" energy. Lifting that pressure allows people the experience of choice. It brings authenticity to effort and builds trust. It grounds all those involved in a sense of shared responsibility for mission, process, and outcomes when people experience that they matter as human beings, not as worker-bees to produce. Amazingly, few things have gone undone over the years. While consulting and teaching, I notice that environments with lots of "should" thinking within staff still experience dropped commitments, missed deadlines, and, most notably, an absence of joy. When working groups offer genuine choice, effectiveness often increases.

Three beautiful byproducts of this approach are a sense of meaning, purpose to work, and a feeling that everyone matters. The sense of shared responsibility naturally emerges from a culture where these values are continually cultivated.

Because language is how we make meaning within and between ourselves, translating "should" has been a longtime project within me, and outside too. In conversations, especially if I am listening to someone mourn an oversight or impact, I offer a translation of the shoulds I hear. For instance, when I hear, "I should have checked with them before acting," I offer, "Do you wish now that you had remembered to check with them?" The reflections are offered as support to metabolize the error as a missed opportunity. I offer these reflections from having translated my own regrets and choices thousands of times. This is an expression of putting the oxygen mask on myself, and of another practice we will look at later: stating the dream, not the nightmare.

"Should" language shows up in me when I am building trust with myself, in a relationship or in a new project or effort. Faithfully noticing it now shows me when I am struggling and need support.

An outcome of this sustained effort is mercy, for myself and for others. As a result, in feedback sessions, conversations, grief circles, and workshops, I frequently hear that people feel safe sharing difficult or shame-inducing situations. What a beautiful gift to offer!

Your Turn: Pay attention to how "should" shows up in your mind and speech. Remember not to be hard on yourself when doing so! When you notice "shoulds" in yourself and others, can you begin to look for the underlying needs?

Cultures of Celebration: An Antidote to Our Miserly Brain

Gratitude is heaven itself.
—William Blake

In the preface of *How to Change the World*, author David Bornstein points to a fundamental social issue: the ratio of problem-focused information to solution-focused information in the media is chronically out of balance. He writes:

> It distorts reality; it is dispiriting; and it deprives people of the knowledge they need to properly assess risks and recognize opportunities. If you were asked to list ten problems facing the world, how long would it take? Two minutes? How long would it take to list ten solutions?

Our brains are extremely efficient at utilizing attention.[66] One outcome of that orientation is that we overlook what is working and offer attention to what doesn't work. Everyone experiences this. Think about a time when a part of your body ceased to function smoothly, like with headaches or broken limbs. Consider how fast you notice when something breaks in your home or office, such as when the power goes out or the internet fails. How much do we think about our health and the working order of mechanical systems when they're functional? Celebrations challenge habits of mind created by either/or thinking, perfectionism, urgency, defensiveness, and the idea of "only one right way."

While the benefits are intuitive, researchers are providing more insight into all the good gratitude and appreciation can do for us. One recent study

---

66. https://www.scientificamerican.com/article/kahneman-excerpt-thinking-fast-and-slow/

shows that positive experiences help sustain our primary relationships.[67] Growing the capacity for gratitude offers emotional and creative energy for positive change in any workspace as well as in family and community commitments. To counter overwhelm and foster energy and positive perspective, we can retrain our attention—personally and organizationally—on practicing gratitude for what works.

To reshape my lens, I use this morning practice: when I wake, I notice and appreciate the smoothly functioning systems in my body and home. For example, I can get out of bed without assistance (unlike my mom) and easily walk to the bathroom, then kitchen. Water and plumbing make cleaning myself a breeze, as does electricity and gas for heat during the winter. An electric hot water kettle and refrigerator create ease in preparing breakfast. Once a week, I listen to the rumble of municipal trucks taking away the neighborhood's recycling and garbage. I turn on my computer and the internet is working. The air outside almost always smells sweet. The list is endless. Noticing all of this propels me into my day feeling slightly stunned with gratitude and humbled with appreciation. It heightens my awareness about the challenges too many of my fellow humans face when these conditions are not present.

The Haudenosaunee people uphold a cultural practice of gratitude, beginning every gathering with a Thanksgiving Address, noticing and thanking the natural systems that sustain life. The invocation is expressed differently each time, based on the speaker's inclination, making it a living expression of praise.[68] They say that each species has a job to do on behalf of creation, and the job of human beings is to express gratitude. In that spirit, every morning I thank trees for air, and breathe. There are twice as many people on earth than when I was born, and far fewer trees. Yet the trees are somehow still doing their "jobs."

In addition to practicing gratitude, we can rewire our brains by being selective about the media we consume. For instance, instead of being immersed in the most outrage-driving headlines the algorithms recommend, I read Nonviolence News—a weekly, award-winning e-publication that collects and shares thirty to fifty global stories of nonviolence in action. The stories feature the problem, the solution, *and* the people who are working

---

67. https://www.rochester.edu/newscenter/online-dating-apps-find-your-love-relationship-science-549422/

68. Freida Jacques discusses the tradition and use of the Thanksgiving Address here: https://www.youtube.com/watch?v=swJs2cGNwIU.

toward that solution. Connecting those three things fosters my capacity to recognize, appreciate, and replicate solutions.

There are many ways to infuse work with practices that counter the trend toward a problem-focus. While working at Bay Area Nonviolent Communication, I invented a title for my role: *director/celebrator*. I did this in part to interrupt the automatic rank handed to someone with the title of executive director, to highlight appreciation as essential to my role, and to strengthen my focus on wins during the long-haul commitment of working for social justice. Each time I explained why I had that unusual title offered a tiny teaching moment to share those principles.

Frequent appreciation of efforts, whether underway or completed, increases groups' collective sense of mattering, of joy, and of accomplishment. Few things are more important for a leader to do than creating an environment that offers those qualities consistently. It reduces the stress, perfectionism, and competition many of us bring to group life.

Consistent attention to appreciation and gratitude offers other benefits too. I once asked Marshall Rosenberg how he developed his remarkably consistent capacity to stay anchored in the present moment. He said that his secret was his longtime habit of using any pause during the day—from standing in lines to waiting at traffic lights—to connect with gratitude.

Gandhi taught and manifested the notion of trusteeship, that all of the gifts we enjoy—including wealth, personal qualities, abilities, and resources of any kinds—are entrusted to us for use on behalf of all life. Seeing oneself as a trustee helps to loosen our attachment to the gifts, boosting our capacity to share and leverage them rather than hoarding or protecting. Practicing gratitude for these resources can help us to remember they are gifts, not burdens.

At the Institute, one way we practiced gratitude was by calling to thank people for their efforts and contributions, regardless of the amount given and without asking for additional support. Many board members grew to delight in making these calls, and the conversations that arose were part of what we shared during meetings.

Your turn: Take two minutes to list what you are grateful for in this present moment. Write as fast or as slow as you like. How do you feel after this exercise? How can you advocate for more opportunities in places you work, worship, and volunteer for appreciation and celebration?

Funds of Knowledge

Even from early interactions, as a visitor and volunteer, I was respected for my funds of knowledge. In a lot of [other] spaces, I had to prove myself, fighting through a lot of male spaces. At the Institute I was immediately trusted. [There was a sense of] "all hands on deck." Everyone has space to contribute.

—Gwen, served as board member then staff at the M. K. Gandhi Institute

Every person has wisdom—their **funds of knowledge**. We honor that knowledge of the world that everyone carries, regardless of their education or their age or their bank account balance. At the Gandhi Institute, we sought to help people experience this for themselves. To paraphrase Myles Horton, education isn't what comes out of the mouth of the educator, it's what is happening in the minds of the students (or workshop participants, or staff, or meeting attendees).

To help people connect to and trust their wisdom, we can ask questions to foster a sense of "best-self activation." This is a term used by researchers to describe the power that is unleashed when people are asked to recall and discuss experiences of success, at any scale. By recalling these past successes, we increase our capacity to engage problems. I routinely utilize questions regarding best-self activation at the start of a new project or a new group. Here's an example: "Remember the best work group (or project, or class) you have ever participated in. What specifically contributed to that experience for you? How did you feel? What qualities and practices from that experience would you like us to consider including for this effort?"

In leadership and facilitation roles, be guided by the questions of others. This creates an opportunity to practice cultural humility by making space for everyone's interests and voices to be included. For instance, during the time I served as director at the Gandhi Institute, reports to the board changed from being written and shared by me to being collaboratively written and shared by staff. During annual meetings with the Gandhi

Institute's board, in addition to written reports, staff invited board members and their families to gather for a lively Q&A session regarding recent efforts.

When we value the knowledge of others, we naturally seek more diversity. There is so much we have to offer one another! I'll say more on the importance of that in chapter 9, in the section on edge effects (page 152).

Your Turn: Think of a time when you learned something unexpected from someone. How did you feel? What are some creative ways to cultivate the conditions where you work, worship, and volunteer for the wisdom each person brings to be sought and shared? Be sure to ask your colleagues too.

Adultism

I appreciated the amount of trust and responsibility I was given as a young person. I felt really empowered and given the space to make mistakes. It was something we gave to students and to staff alike. There were not two sets of rules.
—Jamie, served as staff at the M. K. Gandhi Institute

I loved that you always threw the keys to the youngest people in the room and let them drive—super cool, super empowering. Made so much sense. You trust people to lead like that, and they're ready to go even if they need some skills and resources to step up. People could learn and grow so much faster.
—Thomas, served as board member at the M. K. Gandhi Institute

There's a kind of discrimination that is pervasive and impacts a quarter of our population: adultism. At a training, Dr. Bernard Lafayette described **adultism** as "prejudice against young people as well as favorable bias towards adults and their ideas, activities, and attitudes." I had never conceived of this kind of discrimination before. The moment I heard it, I recognized that bias within myself.

Adultism is at play when older people routinely make decisions for, and without, younger people. It is rampant in education, where students have little to no input into curricula and schedules. Sometimes youth are included as window dressing rather than as genuine partners. I remember many instances when I included young people in decisions and opportunities, with a tinge of self-congratulatory smugness at my open-mindedness. In truth, everyone benefits from the unique perspectives and abilities young people bring. A room without them is missing insights and wisdom that no one else has.

Creating spaces where young people's funds of knowledge are consistently respected can help reveal unconscious adultism in older people who work with them. I remember a conversation at the Institute with a group of young adults who had been involved with gangs and were stepping away from that life—a difficult and at times dangerous task. After finishing a meditation, we discussed the value of feeling peaceful and safe. Instead of presenting ourselves as experts, we asked the group to teach us what they knew. Individuals shared where they found peace and safety in their lives. One person talked about how he used his student city bus pass. When things were not good at home or when conflict looked likely, he would ride the buses until it felt safe—for him and for others—for him to disembark. It was at times the only resource he had, and he used it creatively.

Recognizing adultism shifted and clarified my purpose as a leader. An orientation of service to the next generations through dismantling adultism is one more way to embody cultural humility. Interactions, resource allocation, and decision-making benefit from incorporating youth perspectives. Two examples of the Gandhi Institute's efforts to counter adultism are the Youth Healing Hate Grants and the power of near-peer education, both described in the project stories at the end of this book.

As with any new concept, I can forget my insights around adultism—and other insights—under stress. Studying the ways the unconscious brain races to conclusions without consulting values helps me to be more merciful. None of us asked for the conditioning we received, and we have a responsibility to transform it.

Your Turn: What meaningful connections do you maintain with people of all ages? When you are with younger people, who does most of the talking? How can younger people be more involved and engaged in the places you work, worship, and volunteer? Regardless of your age or position, advocate for this approach.

A Case Study: M. K. Gandhi Institute

Experimentation is another core principle of the Institute. Keep checking with one another, make a decision, pick a time frame, do the experiment, and check back.

—Gwen, served as board member then staff at the M. K. Gandhi Institute

The examples on these pages emerged through years of tiny shifts. For my eleven years there, the Institute served as a laboratory for a series of experiments. It is a very different organization now than when I arrived, and since I left, experimentation has, if anything, increased! Below is an overview of where we started, and from there the choices and decisions we made to integrate nonviolence into our operations.

When I started in 2009, the most useful "artifacts" since the Institute's founding in 1991 by Arun and Sunanda Gandhi were:

- The tagline: educate, embody, and serve
- The connection to the Season For Nonviolence, established by Sunanda and Arun Gandhi
- Items like the Gandhi photo collection that were used to create the Gandhi Cards (see page 170)
- Copies of Arun's book *Legacy of Love*
- The relationship with the University of Rochester which physically hosted the Institute's office at that time and which offered $71,000 in annual support

When I arrived, resources included:

- Half-time administrator and an Americorps member
- Half-time salary for the executive director (me)
- A board that trusted me due to my previous work history
- Arun Gandhi's generous support and friendship

Challenges were:

- Little public recognition, which was sometimes negative
- No physical presence in the community, and very tight quarters in the available space
- An out-of-date website with no back-end access (except to pull the plug)

- No social media presence
- No funding sources except for approximately $40,000 and University of Rochester's support
- No organized donor base or system
- Almost all board members and local supporters were older, white progressives

In the first year I was there, through the dozens of conversations with community members, Arun Gandhi, board members, University of Rochester partners, and potential funders, the nucleus of the Institute's current priorities and values began to emerge. They included:

- A focus on people aged 12–24, to recognize the role they play in social movements globally, and to influence life trajectories by introducing nonviolence to young people.
- The inclusion of sustainability and restorative justice as two of our four pillars, in addition to nonviolence education and racial justice.
- A geographic focus on the Institute's hometown (Rochester, New York) to build a base of support and to have integrity in terms of practicing what we preached, inspired by Gandhi's concept of *swadeshi*, meaning "to focus on local issues, economics, and relationships."

As these priorities were established, practical decisions began to emerge, including:

- Moving to a community-based headquarters while maintaining connection and support for students on the nearby University of Rochester campus. Priorities for our new location included: being on a bus line; having an opportunity to create our own beautiful place and land for growing food; and opportunities for service learning.
- Expanding racial justice efforts, from interpersonal issues to a deeper understanding of implicit bias and systemic racism, which emerged through engagement with numerous projects.
- Developing an inclusive concept of sustainability that positioned nonviolence as an expression of human sustainability, informed by the principles of permaculture. Sharing organic food grown on site with neighbors exemplified the focus on sustainable communities.
- Making Gandhi House vegetarian and prioritizing natural cleaning products. Committing to vegetarian cuisine generated countless valuable conversations about the food industry and about eating a plant-based diet to reduce our collective climate impact.

- Prioritizing local banks and purchases instead of a focus on the "cheapest" option—options that are actually costly from the perspective of global, social, and environmental justice.
- Establishing multiple funding streams to ensure resilience. These came from contracts, grants, fundraising, training fees, and the University of Rochester stipend.
- Initiating a "no one turned away for lack of funds" policy. Informed by Gandhi's concept of trusteeship, we extended this approach to trainings for organizations and to sharing Gandhi House via ongoing partnerships or one time events.[69]
- Utilizing our 501(c)(3) status to serve as fiscal sponsors for projects with related missions. We donated funds and/or volunteered to support the work of others.

Program decisions were initially based on:

- The organization's history of nonviolence education (including the Season For Nonviolence), and a focus on support for incarcerated folks and increasing racial justice.
- Staff interest in applications of nonviolence, including the frameworks of sustainability, restorative justice, and Nonviolent Communication.

Over time they have been increasingly informed by:

- An interest in creating edge effects (see page 152) by experimenting with programs and their evolution, such as "Let's Talk About Hate" workshops, which led to the Youth Healing Hate Grants (see page 171), which inspired Pace e Bene's Changemaker Youth Grants.
- Evolving staff interests, which have included Joanna Macy's *Work That Reconnects*, grief work, Kingian Nonviolence, and others.

Your Turn: What are the underlying principles that shape decisions where you work, worship, and volunteer? Who gave rise to those principles, and are they actively shared now by current stakeholders? How do you experiment with these principles? How do they evolve?

---

69. https://www.mkgandhi.org/articles/trusteeship.htm

Chapter Five Key Ideas

- Characteristics of white supremacy culture—including perfectionism, individualism, urgency, and either/or thinking—influence attitudes, norms, and behaviors whether we realize it or not.
- Exploring underlying beliefs about time is a great team-building opportunity.
- Perfectionism creates fear of mistakes. Seek to create a culture where mistakes are understood as key to learning and innovation.
- "Should" thinking and language are signals of fear, anxiety, and choicelessness. Reframing the language we use fosters autonomy, trust, and shared responsibility.
- A disciplined focus on gratitude increases emotional and creative energy for positive change.
- Connect to existing innate wisdom through questions that foster "best-self activation."
- Dismantling adultism is an expression of cultural humility. Create space for people of all ages to participate as equals.
- Foster a culture of experimentation. Expect to learn about what works and what doesn't together.

Chapter Six

Communication in Groups

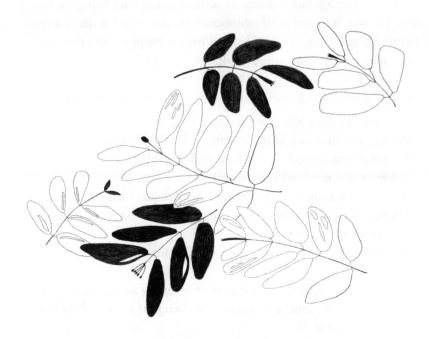

Participation in groups is something we dream about—and dread. The best case scenarios light up our lives and the worst cause us to lose sleep. I have experienced both, and it's a safe bet that you have too.

Think of group work like a boat—not a giant yacht or a sturdy tugboat, but a lifeboat—something with oars and a tiller and not much else. In order to get where you're going, you need to synchronize your oars and hold the tiller steady. The choppier the water, the more blustery the weather, the more you have to work together. The better you are at navigating and working together, the more adventures you can go on. (And the less likely anyone is to fall overboard.) In the best case scenario, group work can bring you into an experience of Beloved Community.

I have experienced Beloved Community during community conversations, daylong prison dialogues, in classes and retreats, and elsewhere. These experiences lead me to see Beloved Community as an energy that arises from a way of being together. In those moments, you can feel the love in the space—which didn't mean we weren't doing hard things or being honest. Honesty and authentic connection set the stage for the emergence of Beloved Community. Trust rises, and trust is *the* protective factor in transformative relationships and work.

Here are some ways of knowing and being to foster great group work:

- Openness to what will emerge
- Willingness to hear and collaborate with others' ideas
- Trust that group wisdom will arise and reveal itself
- Releasing the need to be in control
- Speaking honestly and compassionately in equal measures
- Taking the time you need, rather than the time you have
- Centering on shared purpose
- Bringing music, humor, fun, and creativity into the process

In this chapter, we will explore a variety of listening and speaking practices that foster ease and connection to everyday living, at work and everywhere you encounter people.

Passion Makes for Poor Listening

Listening is an important half of communication that we sometimes forget—it's an active part of it. Sometimes when you're getting feedback, you want to respond immediately. I learned that I can take time to think. We get so scared that we need to have all the answers and respond instantly. Listening requires reflection and listening to yourself.

—Jamie, served as staff at the M. K. Gandhi Institute

All of us struggle with listening. We listen with half an ear. We become excited and interrupt others to express our thoughts. We tune out family, friends, and life partners, expecting them to say the same old things. Under stress, we may bulldoze our way through conversations without hearing the concerns of colleagues, or focus attention on forming a response instead of offering attention to others. All of this churns into a cyclone of feeling unheard, a burning need to express oneself, and patterns of interrupting, frustration, and loneliness—even with our closest people. You may recognize poor listening by physical signals of disconnection, such as multitasking, cameras turned off in virtual meetings, and lack of eye contact.

This challenge is blazingly evident in many organizations, and in community work. In some spaces, I chalk it up to passion—that beautiful, overwhelming emotion that drives us into action. Individuals who take time to participate—especially as volunteers—in community work offer their time and talent because they are enthusiastic or upset and seeking change. You may recognize this in yourself too. We all have stories to tell and knowledge to share. We bring strong notions about how to "fix" the issue, and a desire to express what has driven us to show up. Similar dynamics manifest with friends and family, when old patterns make it difficult to bring our best selves to conversations. Sometimes an attachment to previous solutions, as well as exhaustion and burnout, make it hard to listen. Our old answers can prevent us from listening well and seeking new answers.

Other patterns that obstruct good listening include set-in-stone narratives about others, as well as our own issues and lack of perceived opportunities to express them. These patterns can be addressed by creating norms on how to take turns hearing each other, and giving equitable air time to participants instead of deferring to the leader as routine. Other strategies for engagement include rotating facilitation and other roles, using feedback to reflect on process and outcomes, and ensuring groups cocreate and revisit norms.

Getting mad about habits of poor listening is like getting mad at gravity. It's such a common human tendency that we can free up some emotional energy by deciding to stop expecting something different. Instead of getting irritated when people don't listen, plan for it. When facilitating groups, create opportunities (when possible, in small groups of two or three) for people to start by hearing each other. Ask them questions such as, "What are one or two reasons you chose to be here?" or "What prevents you from being present right now?" Being heard in this way generally refreshes people. It creates an environment that is more focused and productive. In ongoing working groups, whether I am facilitating or in a participant's role, I often call for a pause when it seems that people have ceased to hear each other. I do this at home too. Rather than casting blame, I do this by naming my need to take a minute. Another strategy is to offer something like feedback, such as, "What you just said feels so critical to this effort, thank you. Would you be willing to repeat it?"

Listening is particularly important when topics are painful to discuss, especially as pain is rarely evenly distributed. It is helpful to incorporate some of the following approaches: being transparent, slowing down, acknowledging tension or grief in whatever way seems to fit the moment and the group, and reminding participants that we do not have the same lived experience. As the example above illustrates, coming from gratitude works well. Statements can sound like, "Thank you, your words feel to me like a gift to this group/our work/our relationship." Nonverbal cues like pausing or taking a deep breath also signal careful listening.

Every group has a choice: to stand for process, listening, and clarity, or to focus solely on outcomes. You may find that the former, rather paradox-ically, often contributes to increased trust and efficiency in passionate groups.

Your Turn: What makes it hard for you to listen, no matter how good a listener you know you can be? Is it certain settings, or people, or topics? How can you prepare for those situations, to be more centered and more effective?

Listening as an Act of Love

Good listening is trying to be present as the other talks. . . . Open up your being and just listen. Listen without judgment, with curiosity, awe, discovery. Listen with interest, lean in, and anticipate what this person's going to say next.

—Jonathon, served as staff at the M. K. Gandhi Institute

Who is the best listener you know? I bet a smile came to your face as you thought of them. Listening deeply and attentively is an act of love. If we're lucky, we know at least one or two people who know how to offer this gift. In their presence, we feel seen and understood, welcomed in all our parts, and nourished. From friends to grandparents to therapists and faith leaders, a good listener is a treasure.

We can all be this treasure. Listening is a skill, not a talent. The ability to listen carefully may come naturally to some, but all of us can cultivate it. Can you imagine what life would be like if *everyone* listened well?

As we discussed, most of us struggle to listen at times. Here are a few guesses about why that is:

- As children, we were chastised for not listening when adults wanted us to, so we learned to *appear* to listen.
- Pretending to listen while our minds are on other things can serve as a socially-acceptable escape or coping mechanism.
- Many of us have developed a technologically-acquired attention deficit disorder from the way information is sliced and diced and because our tech is designed to be addictive.[70]

To strengthen listening skills, practice repeating or rephrasing one or two things that the other person just said to you. Reflecting back their words helps to build the muscle of your attention. When attention wanders, be accountable by asking the person if they can repeat what they said, to ensure you are hearing. It's ironic that asking people to repeat what they said can be perceived as good listening, and yet it seems to be the case.

At the Gandhi Institute we developed a workshop called "Listening as an Act of Love and Social Change." Participants discuss the value of being heard and who the best listeners of their acquaintance are. They reflect on what makes for good listening, examine the barriers to listening, and look at what can occur when listening helps to transform judgments and build bridges. Last, participants explore the differences between sympathy, which assumes, and empathy, which inquires.

Participants shared that their takeaways from this workshop included increased clarity regarding the value of listening and increased confidence that each of us has capacity to become a better listener.

Recognizing all of this, we can strive to be "lean of expression" to honor the gift of listening from others. As a practice, I strive to speak (and write!) fewer words than others want to hear. It has been a fascinating, fruitful experiment.

---

70. I found 3,250,000 results when I searched "impacts of technology on human attention span." Here's one on why attention spans are shrinking: https://www.apa.org/news/podcasts/speaking-of-psychology/attention-spans.

Your Turn: What are the barriers to listening in your life? Who are the best listeners you know? Specifically, what do they do and say that offers you that sense of accompaniment and care? Ask some of your close people how well you listen, and listen to what they say!

Becoming Lean of Expression

Gandhi was quite anxious when he was young, reticent and uncertain. In law school, he was so painfully shy that he could not speak in front of groups.[71] I had the reverse issue. My mouth often ran miles ahead of my brain, and my values. Both types of people—and all the varieties in between—can receive support from cocreated group norms. Norms like "move up, move back" help us hear from everyone and foster shared awareness in the group of balancing all the voices in the room. This reminds people who speak easily to speak less, and those who struggle to speak to offer more. We can follow up with feedback at the conclusion of meetings, including celebrating that everyone contributed ideas to the meeting, or offering awareness that some people didn't speak, as a way to build shared accountability.

We can also consider some personal practices around listening and speaking. Here are a few that help me.

Nonviolent Communication helps me look underneath my words, and those of others, for the underlying feelings and needs. Through it, I learned to translate judgments into observations and to seek ways to ask for what I need, rather than expecting my listener to be a mindreader. My teachers Rita Herzog and Marshall Rosenberg suggested a practice of speaking forty words (or less) before stopping to check for understanding from others—a great way of making sure I don't get off track from the heart of the matter.

The discipline of this approach leads me to experience Nonviolent Communication as a mindfulness practice rather than a communication process.

Restorative practices teach me about trust and patience in groups.[72] In group spaces, I often experience surges of excitement or frustration that

71. Eknath Easwaran, *Gandhi the Man: The Story of His Transformation*, 19.
72. Restorative practices are a field of social science, drawn from indigenous cultures worldwide, that studies how to strengthen relationships between individuals and communities. I have had direct experiences with applications in schools, organizations, faith communities, courts, and prisons, and have yet to find a place where the approach does not work.

translate into an urgency to speak, even before becoming clear about what I truly want to say. Sitting in circles and in thousands of meetings, I learned to notice—not act on—those energy surges. Now this noticing allows me to speak with less frequency, more clarity, and fewer words. Frequently, when I keep silent, someone else articulates the same point.

Meditation practices help me to "mind the gap" between the stimulus of hearing others and my first response, which is often overwhelmed or grumpy. I let that first response wash over me like a wave, then look for what the second or third wave brings. To support the practices of slowing down and being more thoughtful, I use tools: having something to hold (like a stone), or something to play with (like a soft toy), or an image that inspires me to be my best self. These days, I keep a photo of myself at six months old pinned to the edge of my desktop computer. That wise baby smiles at me encouragingly all day long!

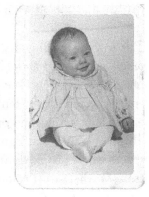

These practices help me to become lean of expression. It's an approach that has many ripple effects. First, it's respectful. It allows others time to speak and voice their thoughts. It lets me take in the gift of what they're saying. It honors the preciousness of their attention by distilling my comments into what's most important to convey. It's another way to practice cultural humility—by not presuming that I have the most interesting ideas, or deserve more speaking time. Last but not least, I say fewer things I regret, which does wonders for my peace of mind! Ultimately, being lean of expression is an act of love for myself and others.

Your Turn: Pay attention to the number of words you speak in different situations. What conditions prompt more words in some settings, and fewer words in others? After collecting some data on yourself, are there changes you would like to make?

Separating Understanding and Agreement

I think about how important empathy has been when I've been in conflict and I'm stuck. The sense that someone—ideally the person I'm upset with, but someone—is understanding and validating what is going on for me has often been what I've needed to be willing to think about something else, to move past being stuck. I see that playing out so frequently in the multitudes of conversations I have with kids who are in conflict.

—Spero, served as staff at the M. K. Gandhi Institute

I have witnessed a dynamic within myself, and noticed one in others, that contributes to polarization in many spaces: we are reluctant to acknowledge that we understand what someone is saying if we don't agree with them.

This way of signaling disagreement is costly. I have found consistently that *people are hungrier for understanding and respect than for agreement* on their perspective or idea. One way we can make sure people feel understood and respected is to listen carefully for as long as it takes while checking for understanding, and only then ask to share a perspective that differs. This builds trust and signals that the individual matters, and it is helpful in spaces where people don't know each other, with new employees or volunteers, or where trust is low.[73]

Reflecting on the times I've noticed myself refusing to acknowledge someone's meaning, it has often been related to a lack of centeredness (which is why the inside job of nonviolence is so critical). Especially when the content of what is being shared is difficult, find and use practices to stay centered, like mindful breath, asking for a pause to take in what the other person needs beneath their words, or silently reciting a meaningful verse or mantra. Norms that value every person's contribution can support anyone in a group to name a dynamic they are noticing.

A powerful experience of leaning on this approach, and asking others to do the same, came from facilitating a dialogue with my women's group, Shades of Sisterhood. There was tension in the group between Black and Jewish women about the relative historic harm that each group experienced. After volunteering to facilitate the dialogue we agreed to have on the topic, I asked the group to focus on understanding, to slow down and, as best as possible, drop the wish for agreement. This specific request supported engagement, calling upon the shared care and interest in learning that group members have in common.

---

73. Attorney, author, and mediator Gary Friedman describes this approach as "looping," a key strategy in conflict resolution. For more of Friedman's work, visit his organization The Center for Understanding in Conflict at https://understandinginconflict.org/.

Signaling understanding is such a powerful approach that violence inter-rupters, crisis responders, and hostage negotiators use it to de-escalate the threat of violence. When a person is agitated, furious, or flying off the handle, indicating that you hear and comprehend what they're saying is one of the fastest ways to cool off the situation. When people don't feel heard, what do they do? They talk louder, faster. They shout more intensely. And then, if they still don't feel like you're listening, they can lash out. This is also true in less volatile situations. Especially if you don't agree with the points they're making, expressing understanding signals respect and care. When the other person or group is braced for a fight and instead receives listening and respect, the table can be set for learning and engagement.[74]

Your Turn: Can you separate understanding from agreement? Practice while watching movies or TV, or with conflicts you are not participating in. In which relationships and spaces do you find it hard to do this? Where is it easy?

Intention and Impact

As we discussed in chapter 4, intention and impact are two different things. You may *intend* to cheer someone up with a delicious chocolate-walnut cake, but if they're allergic to nuts, your *impact* is a life-threatening danger. Understanding this distinction is important for handling conflicts skillfully with a range of people, from kids (who only wanted to have a good time jumping on the waterbed before it broke) to coworkers (who assumed their colleague was willing—or even able—to pull an all-nighter with them to meet the deadline).

When hurt has occurred, those who caused it frequently want to be under-stood for their innocent intentions. People on the receiving end want to be understood for the impact of the behavior, especially if this is not the first time they've experienced this kind of harm from you or others. The framework of intention and impact helps us navigate these moments.

For example, when my stepdad responds to questions for my mother during doctor visits, I say something like: "I believe you intend to support mom by answering these questions. However, that doesn't give her a chance to speak for herself. Can you give her time to respond?"

---

74. Gwen Olton offers strategies and insights for resolving community conflicts in her outstanding book, *From Conflict to Community: Transforming Conflicts without Authorities.*

Marshall Rosenberg modeled utilizing roleplays as a strategy for learning, which is what I did when I spoke with someone who works for a nonprofit organization. She is Black and felt frustrated when an older, white male donor offered help in a way that she experienced as well-intentioned and demeaning. We did a roleplay of how she could engage and hopefully change these dynamics.

> Her: I am glad to have a chance to continue to speak about ways we can work together, and I am grateful for your interest in our work. I also feel excited about the resources you named to support the project. At the same time, I was troubled by a couple of things from our first conversation. Because I want our work together to have as strong a foundation as possible, I wonder if you would be willing to take a couple of minutes before we speak about other things to chat about this. Are you open to doing this?

> Him: Sure, I'm okay with that.

> Her: Thank you. After reflecting on our conversation, I realized I was troubled a couple of times, especially when you appeared to assume that I needed support in understanding how to do my job. Even while trusting your overall intention to contribute, I want you to know that the effect on me was quite challenging.

> Him: I was just helping.

> Her: I get that. I get that your overall intention is to support me. And it brought up all kinds of reactions in me because of how often this happens that a white man assumes a Black woman doesn't know her business. Or assumes that you are better at things, or have some special wisdom that I need from you. I really want to avoid an unconscious replication of that colonial dynamic for both of us. How is it to hear this?

This was our roleplay. In real life, she decided one request she could make was to agree that they would check in about this dynamic going forward, for ongoing feedback and to build trust. Walking toward the conflict as she did created a deeper connection with this person and built a habit she could turn to for similar dynamics in other situations.

Exploring intention and impact is not always difficult—sometimes it reveals sweet surprises. For example, it may have been no big deal for you to pull over and help someone fix their flat tire, but the impact for them may be huge. Maybe they're trying to get to an important appointment, or maybe your support boosted their faith in humanity on that particular day. Later we'll explore how important feedback processes are. In my experience, many of us are unaware of how our words and actions powerfully, positively impact others.

Your Turn: Think of a time when your intention and impact were misaligned. Were you able to resolve it? Is there something you would have liked to have done differently? How have you communicated when others made choices that impacted you? Is there something you could do differently?

State the Dream, Not the Nightmare

We stay in touch. Other jobs I've had, we were work buddies at work but not outside. At the Institute, it feels like a Beloved Community. We're in constant contact to support each other. If someone's trying to move, we help. If someone's going on vacation, we help. It's a culture of asking for the support you need. And of being willing to say, "No, I can't," and feel comfortable and confident that you can say no without being judged. Everybody's a leader in the space.

—Jonathon, served as staff at the M. K. Gandhi Institute

People are often surprised, inspired, and motivated by hearing someone propose a vision or articulate shared values. The roleplay shared earlier illustrates this transformational approach summarized by Nonviolent Communication teacher Rita Herzog: *state the dream, not the nightmare.* In the role play in the previous section, my friend mentioned "a strong foundation for working together" as a reason why both of them could be committed to dealing with the troublesome dynamics going on. When we pair feedback with a vision, we empower creativity and willingness to make change.

Here are examples of stating the dream, not the nightmare:
- Would you be open to scheduling regular time for feedback, rather than holding off until an issue occurs?
- Can we ask if anyone wants to help, instead of assuming they don't?

Clarity regarding shared values and vision creates an on-ramp for moving toward challenging subjects. As a discipline, at home, work, and elsewhere, you can practice gaining this clarity by stating the dream, or asking yourself, "What's your *why* for this project or effort?" Try following these three steps:

- First, articulate what you'd like to see instead of beginning with a focus on problems, and support others to do the same.
- Second, ask for and offer space for others to receive acknowledgement for the frustration or anger with the challenges at hand.
- Third, begin to look for strategies that meet as many needs as possible. In Nonviolent Communication, we call this the "request phase." It focuses on making requests in positive action language instead of indicating what is *not* wanted.

Following these steps allows us to get clear, so that we aren't handing the other person an emotional or logistical puzzle to sort out on our behalf. Sometimes the process described above is more circular and messy than linear, and that's OK—as long as all three steps happen.

Your Turn: What would you put on your list of best ways to approach group work? Think of your all-time best group experience. What qualities or practices make it stand out for you now? What conditions and dynamics prevent you from experiencing those qualities in more settings?

Chapter Six Key Ideas

- Authentic connection and trust set the stage for groups to embody Beloved Community.
- Passion, stress, and feeling unheard make it hard to listen. Foster listening by slowing down, acknowledging tension, and centering gratitude.
- Listening is a skill, not a talent.
- Nonviolent Communication, restorative practices, and meditation lend support in speaking mindfully.
- Prioritizing understanding over agreement is an important way to let others know they matter, especially during disagreements or conflicts.
- When hurt occurs, attending to intention and impact supports feeling understood and building deeper connections.
- State the dream, not the nightmare. Pairing feedback with vision empowers creativity and willingness to make change.

Chapter Seven
Experiments with Conflict

The complicated truth is that many of the oppressed are also oppressors, and many of the oppressors are also oppressed—nonviolent confrontation is the only form of confrontation that allows us to respond realistically to such complexity.

—Barbara Deming

It catches you off guard when you come in with a lot of heat and fear, and are met with empathy. . . . Initially that was such a shock that—wow this is possible, instead of defensiveness or combativeness.

—Jamie, served as staff at the M. K. Gandhi Institute

Reflecting on work with Dr. Martin Luther King Jr. and others over decades of activism, Dr. Bernard Lafayette shared the following insight during a visit with Gandhi Institute staff: what most often impedes progress are challenges with colleagues, more than problems with those we regard as opponents. I have heard similar reflections from others, and experienced those dynamics myself.[75] I believe that resentment and unwillingness to give and receive feedback are the most frequent issues.

While experiencing this kind of infighting can be frustrating, recognizing it as a significant obstacle is empowering. After all, we have more influence over the atmosphere and efforts we undertake with colleagues than any other group, regardless of our role. In large systems, where a sense of powerlessness often prevails, the way we work together and the way we disagree with one another offer a powerful vehicle for change.

Conflict and friction are common in groups. Knowing this, how can we operationalize love, acceptance, and safety in order to nurture effective groups and organizations?

Conflict is inevitable in group work. Two colleagues can't agree on the font for the new flier. Your partner doesn't like the timeline for the project at hand. Another coworker expresses frustration with not being heard in staff meetings. No one agrees on budget priorities.

Rather than letting disagreements fester, we can practice harnessing their potential. When working with others, even those who we regard as like-minded, we can be surprised and disappointed that conflicts arise. Annoyance and resentments occur as we bump into each other's styles and strategies. Fostering skills to harness the energy of our conflicts in a timely way is a form of power that every one of us can claim. This chapter contains skills, practices, and approaches to do just that.

---

75. In an article called "Building Resilient Organizations," organizer Maurice Mitchell calls these in-group dynamics "the small war." Be sure to read this article which highlights many themes from this book: https://forgeorganizing.org/article/building-resilient-organizations.

Walking Toward Conflict[76]

Sometimes conflict is needed in order for people to understand each other.
—Natasha, served as staff at the M. K. Gandhi Institute

Nonviolence makes the world safe for conflict.
—Dorothy Day

When a conflict nears, many of us bolt in the opposite direction. We avoid dealing with it, maybe by ignoring it and hoping it goes away. Sometimes that works, and sometimes the problem grows bigger. This experience feeds our fear of conflict, especially since our memories retain negative experiences more consistently than positive.

What if we were not afraid to walk toward conflict? When you can't swim, it's sensible to be afraid of the water. But if you know how to swim, you're eager to dive in. The same can be true for dealing with conflict. When you know conflict can be an opportunity to deepen relationships and you have the skills to navigate it, you may even be excited to move toward it.

It's not easy to walk toward conflict. Even after years of inner—and outer—work, I struggle to transform my conditioning. Examining your personal story of conflict offers insight with which you can change how you approach conflict. Growing up, my family dodged difficult conversations and avoided open conflict. Problems were not discussed until someone blew up, often under the influence of alcohol. I have one vivid childhood memory of an argument my parents had at dinner. I was ten or eleven, still small enough to swing my legs under my chair. It seemed like a small spat over an inconsequential issue, but suddenly, my father snatched his plate off the table and hurled it on the floor. The plate shattered. I gathered my three younger siblings and got out of that room as fast as I could.

I wish my parents had been taught to discuss and resolve disagreements with more skill. It would have positively altered the course of their lives, and mine. With training and daily commitment, I practice nonviolence to transform this inherited pattern. Moments in my life that I most celebrate relate to peacefully standing for my values during conflicts, and being useful to others in the midst of their conflicts and difficulties.

---

76. "Walking toward conflict" is a phrase coined by Dominic Barter: https://muse.jhu.edu/pub/4/article/469532.

Below is a list of my top conflict strategies. They work in part because people *can* change their opinions, hearts, and minds—and it turns out that believing people can resolve conflicts helps to create the possibility that they will.[77]

- Walk toward conflicts when they're small.
- It's okay to acknowledge that you have a challenge before you have a solution.
- Play with your language about conflict. If you notice a fear of having or bringing up "conflicts," use words like "dilemma" or "challenge" or "pattern" to circumvent that fear.
- Choose your moment for addressing issues. Try to pick a time when you and the other person are more likely to feel spacious and resourced, and less likely to feel pressured and stressed.
- Make sure everyone involved knows they matter.
- Increase your personal support system. Set up conversations with friends who share your values (conflict resolution vs. conflict escalation) as a regular routine instead of waiting for emergencies. It's too hard to ask for help when we feel stuck or down.
- Remember: empathy before education.
- Double check for comprehension—what looks like resistance is often a lack of clarity.
- In highly charged moments, separate understanding from agreement. Feeling understood is the deepest need, even more than agreement.
- When routinely challenged by someone, find something they love and remember it as a way to humanize them.
- Take an actual walk with this person. Research is demonstrating that physically walking with people while working out an issue supports both learning and resolution.[78]

After years of practicing with these techniques, when a conflict comes up, I feel like an EMT or medical professional responding to a heart attack. I'm skilled and prepared to deal with the situation, so I move toward it with less fear. Here's a story of a time I walked toward conflict, using some of the strategies described above.

---

77. Peter Coleman, *The Way Out: How to Overcome Toxic Polarization*, 99. Harboring the belief that people, groups, and situations might change makes it conceivable to see and realize possible solutions to problems. In addition to Coleman's book, the accompanying website is loaded with wisdom on this topic. https://www.thewayoutofpolarization.com/
78. https://pubmed.ncbi.nlm.nih.gov/28481583/

One day, I noticed a pickup truck just down the street from the Gandhi Institute, with a flagpole flying a large Confederate flag. It felt like an affront and a threat to the historically Black neighborhood we were in.

Breathing deeply and muttering a quick prayer, I approached the white driver of the truck who was talking to another white man. I was cautious as I knew that connecting in front of an audience could lead to more of a performative exchange than one of any real meaning. I started by telling him I was curious about the flag and asked him if he would be willing to talk to me about it. He seemed surprised and said yes, his courtesy possibly prompted by mine.

I asked what the flag meant to him and he responded, "It's an American flag." I said I was surprised by that and that I had met people from the South who thought of it as a regional flag, so I asked if he was from the South. He responded "No, I'm from here," he said. I told him that my husband had ancestors who fought on both sides of the Civil War, making it an area of interest in our family. He brightened and said, "Yes, I've heard that that was true of many people." I said that from what I understood, that flag stood for a time when our country was divided and deeply troubled, so I did not think it was a flag that stood for the whole country. He answered that he was an Army veteran who loved flags. He showed me a variety of flags that he had in the truck, including a tattered American flag. I mentioned that a number of people in the neighborhood where we were standing were also veterans. Even though I was clear that I did not approve of the flag, I was trying to be conscious to model respect, concern, and curiosity. I was aware that this was an opportunity to have the kind of exchange that former white supremacists like Arno Michaelis and Frank Meeink[79] report were influential in helping them question and rethink their beliefs.

I thanked him for the time, and as I walked away, he took the flag down.

We can practice walking toward conflict by moving toward what makes us uncomfortable. In my twenties and thirties, I participated in volunteer opportunities that often felt intense, courtesy of the amazing faith

79. Arno's organization is Life After Hate: https://www.lifeafterhate.org/. Frank cowrote a book called *Autobiography of a Recovering Skinhead: the Frank Meeink Story*. Both are incredible resources about leaving violent extremism.

community that continues to nourish me and thousands of others still.[80] These included serving in an overnight shelter for unhoused people, becoming a caregiver in a hospice and, when my daughter Molly was a toddler, caring for women and their children with AIDS. I often low-level dreaded going because of the unpredictability and intensity that could show up. And I almost always left with humility, gratitude, and awe for humanity, our resilience and insights. I feel the same combination often while walking toward difficult conversations like the one described above.

Your turn: Have you ever intervened in a conflict that was not yours? What did you learn? When you reflect on conflicts with colleagues, which of the strategies listed above would offer the most support?

Costs of Unresolved Conflict

The waters must be troubled.
—Howard Thurman

The question of how we can find an answer that works for everyone is something I was teaching at the Institute. What stands out for me, as a moment from teaching a principle to using it, was when I had a chance to resolve an issue in real time with the school principal in the midst of lunchtime cafeteria chaos. It turned us from opponents to collaborators.
—Matt, served as staff at the M. K. Gandhi Institute

Internal, interpersonal, and systemic conflicts don't vanish on their own or disappear if we ignore them. They often worsen, fester, and continue to cause harm. There are costs to unresolved conflicts.

We may avoid interpersonal conflict because we feel unprepared, or fearful. Sometimes, there are emotional risks, but there can also be risks to finances, social status, or physical safety. In other situations, many of us worry that we'll make matters worse by trying.

For whatever reason, many of us forget that there is another side of the "balance sheet." We calculate the risks of getting involved, but we forget

---

80. https://spirituschristi.org. I began attending in 1985, delighted it was my great grandparents' church where my grandfather and siblings attended grade school. My husband and I first held hands during a service there in 1989.

the costs of ignoring or prolonging the conflict. In my life, these costs include painful cut-offs from friends and family, resentment, pain, and regret. I notice much of my mental and emotional bandwidth is used up when I try to manage my reactions to a conflict without trying to resolve it. In organizations, the results of ignoring conflict include low performance, tension, quitting, projects failing, stress, dysfunction throughout the group, and more. I wish we measured and calculated those costs! Think of all those resources we could use for other things—like more paid vacation time for all, or shorter work weeks with full pay.

Ignoring conflict in order to avoid more conflict is what Johan Galtung called negative peace. Negative peace is the absence of overt violence, verbal or physical. He named positive peace as the absence of indirect or structural violence. Creating this positive peace requires more than just ending harm— it also calls for building a system where everyone's needs are met. This doesn't happen by accident, but asks us to walk towards conflict and invite the other person to work with us.

Beyond conflicts at the interpersonal level, we need support and community to be courageous about dealing with conflicts at the societal level. As people like Dr. King and Myles Horton taught, if we are not actively struggling against oppression, then oppression is moving in and growing. Injustice and oppression are not static.

So, what are the benefits of trying to resolve a conflict, even when it goes badly or differently than you would like? For me, these include honoring my own values, remembering that conflict is often a midwife for change, and preferring to feel positive regret (mourning and learning) instead of shame or remorse. I rate effort and wholeheartedness highly on the "plus" side of the conflict balance sheet, which generally tips me into action during inter-personal tensions. Another benefit is in the critical learning that comes from trying, and sometimes failing. Life ensures our development by generously providing plenty of opportunities for us to learn and grow.

Lately, I've been leading sessions to help groups plan for conflict. When people plan for conflict together, it builds community, trust, courage, and accountability. It increases their capacity to relax with the inevitable complexity of group life. Note that once a conflict plan or system is in place, for a while more conflicts will likely show up. This is because of a backlog of tensions that have been suppressed or unacknowledged that are now coming forward. Hearing about them is a sign of health returning, not a problem—like the pins and needles feelings in our limbs when they have gone numb and are recovering from numbness.

Your turn: Think of a few unresolved conflicts. Choose one, and make a conflict "balance sheet." On one side is the projected value of trying to resolve or restore. On the other side, make a list of reasons to take no action. Include fears, values, and other variables. Is there new insight from this exercise? Are there patterns you notice from other situations, or from your family?

Responding to Challenges

Experience gave me perspective about the usefulness and the need for restorative work. Even though the outcome still felt messy, there was movement in the process. That's another lesson that felt useful later as a facilitator, to not have the goal that everyone walk away smiling and be happy. Instead, to have the goal of engagement.
—David, served as staff at the M. K. Gandhi Institute

There have been many opportunities to engage with groups and individuals who did not like a stance we took, or a decision that I made while serving as the Gandhi Institute's director. Here is one of many examples of how we approached those moments.

As part of our commitment to nonviolence and to sustainability, the M. K. Gandhi Institute cooked and served vegetarian food at our events. Though we received some complaints from meat eaters, these were minor compared to the distress expressed by a local vegan group when they learned that we had begun to keep chickens and share eggs with neighbors. (The chickens had a lifelong home with us; they were not going to be eaten.) I became averse to eating chicken the first time I held one and—with a shock—recognized the bone structure of their chest from having cooked so many. We wondered if others might become equally convinced through the power of firsthand experience. Many children and adults who visited the Institute had never met a chicken until it was on their plate!

At the same time, sharing fresh organic eggs (as well as produce from our gardens) was a part of our relationship-building with our neighbors. The

Gandhi Institute is located within a neighborhood that the USDA has declared a food desert—an area without clear access to a grocery store beyond the limited, expensive options in corner stores. People in the neighborhood routinely experience poor food options and, consequently, poorer health; it's part of the structural violence of poverty. We saw sharing eggs as non-harming to the hens, and food sharing as a time-honored, cross-cultural means of building stronger relationships in the community.

Unfortunately, the chickens became a source of tension with the vegan group. We responded to the expressed concerns, explaining our perspective and strategy. Additionally, a young staff member who had grown up close by and knew hunger frequently as a child offered to meet with the group to clarify our thinking. It was a generous offer for a young Black man to make to a group of white middle-class progressives. They met, but these efforts did not appear to change their perspective.

We resisted the pressure. We felt committed to the reasons that compelled us to keep chickens in the first place. We also felt that serving vegetarian food was a sufficient "ask" for staff and visitors. Many of the people we worked with had not encountered a vegetarian diet before; giving up meat (even for a meal) was a stretch. To my knowledge, we were the only youth space in the area that stuck to a vegetarian policy. Among the many groups we hosted and worked with, we felt that vegetarian food was our best approach.

Meanwhile, some months went by and disaster struck. Raccoons broke into the chicken house and killed each of the five chickens. At this point, the birds had been named and lovingly cared for by the team and neighbors (including our friend and neighbor David Dornford, a Vietnam veteran who visited each day and petted them). The following spring, with competing priorities for attention and resources, we let go of keeping the chickens.

Looking back, I would wish for increased capacity to slow down and attend to the concerns. I would ask for support from more people so we could increase the dialogue flow. Even with the frustration of never fully resolving the issue directly, it is an important principle for healthy conflict and healthy communities to be curious and to care about what mattered to the "other side." I can easily imagine that this group may have felt hurt and indignant that their values and contributions were not more influential in setting policy.

Challenge and conflict offer a chance to reflect on *why* we hold certain beliefs. There is so much that can be learned when the focus remains on continuing to see the people "on the other side" as human beings and potential teachers, rather than as threats to our self esteem or peace of mind. Bringing creativity to conflict is a core principle of nonviolence.

Your Turn: Think of a time you or a group you were in experienced a challenge from others. What happened? What did you learn? In hindsight, what do you wish you/the group had known to do differently?

Connection: Conflict and Creativity

Movements are born of critical connections rather than critical mass.
—Grace Lee Boggs

Conflict becomes easier to navigate when we study, rather than judge, the dynamics of violence. Learning to relax more with the presence and the inevitability of conflict, we can learn more from witnessing and being in conflicts ourselves. Consequently, a most useful insight emerges: conflict and creativity are two sides of the same coin. What flips the coin is the presence, or absence, of trust.

When the coin of conflict and creativity tilts toward trust, it is possible to have "fun fights." These creative divergences enliven us, bring fresh ideas, and deepen the wisdom in our endeavors. *Strong opinions, loosely held* is a bit of wisdom I've gleaned from the *Barefoot Guide 5: Mission Inclusion.*[81] Holding views loosely opens new perspectives, and enables genuine collaboration.

During the remodel of the abandoned house that is now the home of the Gandhi Institute, there were opportunities for "fun fights" with board members, the volunteer interior designer, and the contractor, especially regarding ideas about which colors for the rooms and house itself would feel "peaceful." Staff at the Institute were on the same page—we had a clear vision of a colorful space, inspired by the sensibilities of Indian culture. This meant choosing rich, bold colors and steering away from the default cool neutrals common to so many public spaces in the US. Those who

---

81. https://www.barefootguide.org/barefoot-guide-5---mission-inclusion.html

didn't help create this vision would push back: How could we consider deep red a peaceful color? They were earnest and laughing—these were strong opinions loosely held, allowing them to delight in the differences between our views. All in all, the stakes were low, and this was a great opportunity to have fun with conflict.

Every team I have ever participated in has conversations like fun fights regarding decision making. The more trust there is, the more freedom exists to disagree, learn from and about one another, frequently laugh, and choose *together*.

One key to maintaining trust and staying grounded in the face of conflict is studying the dynamics of conflict. At work, at home, and in the community, everyone benefits from this learning, especially since so many of us were not taught these crucial skills. Commit to ongoing learning about conflict as a way to become more useful in every aspect of life.

Your Turn: In what work and professional spaces do you feel most free to be yourself, relaxed, and creative with other people? What happens in those spaces that enables you to experience this?

Structure, Relationship, Skills

Having a feedback process with components and a framework, it was like having training wheels or bumpers on the bowling lane. It helped to lubricate difficult moments, specifically difficult feedback when there's a power differential. It contributed to increased trust, sharing, and letting go of resentments.
—David, served as staff at the M. K. Gandhi Institute

To address conflict, most organizations and groups rely on structures, both legal and organizational, that were not created, or consented to, by current team members. They may make detailed plans for how staff can call for a meeting and for a moderator to deal with a problem, and wonder why no one seems to know about or use the system. Sometimes policies and structures inadvertently make matters worse as a result of the amount of time required, and because of a default legal response to avoid/minimize contact with the other—even when they sit side by side in an office! Structures alone are particularly ineffective as many conflicts

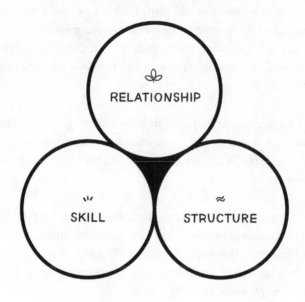

From "Healing Resistance" by Kazu Haga,

are a mix of interpersonal and systemic issues, yet are primarily viewed as interpersonal.[82]

When groups rely solely on relationships for decision making and conflict resolution, some people will deal with their issues, and many will not. If the parties are alienated, or struggle with unequal power or position, the issue is more likely to fester or worsen. As for skill, managers are taught to think that training will fix issues that arise. They book a workshop and then wonder why people still struggle.

Structure, relationship, and skills are the key ingredients that are needed to bake good conflict processes into your organization.[83] If all three are cultivated then you're setting up more people for success. If you cocreate structures like protocols, guidelines, formal mediation, and feedback processes, and if those agreements are renewed at whatever interval make sense to your team, you are on your way. Other steps to success include a thorough orientation for new people by leadership and by peers to these

---

82. We can cultivate a sense of gratitude and hope for the growing understanding from science about how our brains process information, how trauma influences us, and how our emotional IQ changes depending on what is happening in the present moment. This type of information can be used to increase collective well-being and effectiveness to reform policies and practices. One of many great resources: *What Happened to You?* by Perry and Winfrey, listed in resources at the end of this book.

83. This diagram of relationship, skill, and structure is based on the original graphic from *Healing Resistance* by Kazu Haga—an image from Miki Kashtan. We are teaching each other!

ways of knowing, being, and doing, as well as an identified quiet, aesthetically pleasing space for holding conflict processes.

OK, let's state the dream: you have built relationships and trust through regular check-ins, icebreakers, sharing meals, and rotating roles so different people get the chance to work together, breaking up silos. People are trained in active listening, Nonviolent Communication, restorative practices, facilitation, and de-escalation skills. When issues arise, they're equipped to dig in, mourn mistakes and impacts, generate solutions, and keep learning together. All of this effort and infrastructure is communicated during hiring processes and included in evaluations to communicate the commitment to creating the best possible environment. These actions lead to attracting ever-better candidates for your team, both paid and volunteer, and mean that people do not want to leave.

Put your vision to work by spending time on structures of support like building agreements and processes for responding to harm in a timely, clear way.

Your Turn: Use the framework of skill/relationship/structure to inventory your organization, department, or team for a refreshed analysis of what to celebrate and what is missing, and then begin to implement.

Creating Space for Conflict

The challenge of our time is to mobilize people to make change without dehumanizing one another. Not just because it's morally right, but because it works.
—Amanda Ripley

In a circle, three people who experienced the same set of circumstances saw what happened completely differently. It opened my eyes to how naive we can be to understanding other people's viewpoints. By the time we got to the end, everyone's body relaxed. . . . We don't all get to the same place at the same time.
—Natasha, served as staff at the M. K. Gandhi Institute

Along with tools for teaching constructive conflict, making safe places to have conflicts fosters human creativity. Dominic Barter speaks of the need for physical spaces for communities to hold and acknowledge conflict. As he says, "We can predict we will be hungry every day, so we build homes with kitchens. In the same way, we can predict we will see things differently from one another. We need spaces in community life where conflicts can be swiftly and productively held." [84]

From the Gandhi Institute's work in schools in Rochester and elsewhere, I see that these spaces need to be places that people will access for themselves, not be sent to by authority figures, implying punishment rather than a choice to understand and transform conflict. One example of these spaces in Rochester schools are Help Zones. These physical spaces help model the possibility for transformative conflict within every head and heart. [85]

Help Zones are rooms, large or small, dedicated to caring for relationships and normalizing the resolution of conflicts, which may also be large or small. There's nothing fancy about it: a table, a few chairs, a box of tissues, inspiring wall art, comfortable furniture. It's an area where students know they can invite each other to resolve disputes. Creativity is at the heart of these spaces. For instance, one wise colleague, Alex, kept nail polish on hand. She would offer to paint the nails of middle school students during a conflict as a strategy for refocusing attention and slowing the parties down while they waited for their nails to dry.

While your space for dialogue and conflict does not have to look any particular way, I recommend incorporating elements that most easily help people feel welcome. Plants, art work, and a door that closes and offers some privacy are a few key ingredients. Maybe your Help Zone can be drawn on the playground with a piece of chalk. Maybe a particular space at your work could be routinely utilized to host these conversations, to build a recognized rhythm into how your team navigates difficult moments. Use the funds of knowledge of colleagues to decide what will work best.

These spaces can look like the inspiring dedicated restorative circle space at Canticle Farm, an intentional community in Oakland, California, founded by my friends Anne and Terry Symens-Bucher. [86] The conflict

84. Listen to this interview featuring Dominic chatting with Gandhi staff members, reflecting on building spaces for conflict: https://gandhiinstitute.org/2023/11/14/interviewing-dominic-barter/.
85. For data and student reflections on this work, see https://gandhiinstitute.org/school-climate-transformation/.
86. https://canticlefarmoakland.org/

room at Canticle is centrally located, beautifully painted, and contains books on mindfulness and conflict. At the Gandhi Institute, we held those conversations in our meditation space, or in the garden. As mentioned earlier in the section "Walking Toward Conflict," taking a walk, ideally outdoors, is a good approach borne out by research. Conflicts benefit from beauty as well as care.

Proactively supporting colleagues by dedicating time, space, and process to harness the power of conflict offers tangible proof to individuals within organizations—whether it be a company, a school, or a faith community— that their well-being matters. It also normalizes conflict as a human dynamic that can be utilized to contribute to, not detract from, purpose, connection, and effectiveness.

Your Turn: What are the dedicated spaces in your life that nourish your sense of connection to self and others? Could you advocate for a planned approach to hold conflicts at work and in other places you spend time, including a space to honor the effort and the people?

The Efficiency of Trust

We're showing trust. It's a longer-term approach that puts relationships at the forefront, which is consistent with what we're peddling. It makes for richer relationships. Good things derive from that approach. It allows us to go to donors and supporters in good faith asking for support to invest in our people, which makes us more effective.

—Erin, served as staff at the M. K. Gandhi Institute

Trust is a form of relational wealth in every setting, especially if we are privileged to serve as leaders or managers. It is, in my opinion, the single biggest asset in relationships and groups. I have seen groups with very big budgets suffer—sometimes even fail—when trust was not tended to, including at schools, nonprofits, and departments within larger entities. Best of all, it is *within your capacity* to grow it.

When reflecting on the state of trust in places you work, look for the following signals of the absence of trust: people are unwilling or fearful to speak; they skip or avoid work, meetings, and other commitments; there is a general unwillingness to extend empathy or grace to others.

Here's an exercise borrowed from Steven Covey Jr.: Take one minute to think of someone you trust. What's it like when you make decisions together, or when you disagree? Notice and describe to yourself how you feel in your body when you think of that person. (Safe, warm, relaxed, easeful—what words would you use to describe the feeling?) Then, think of someone who you used to trust but no longer do. (Tense, uneasy, guarded, nervous—what comes up for you?) Notice the difference between the two.

Without trust, the work of minutes becomes hours or days . . . or never happens.

Here are some practices and principles that, among other things, help to create, sustain, and at times re-establish trust.[87] Note the overlap with the top strategies for conflict shared from the section "Walking Toward Conflict" in this chapter.

- Conflict in high-trust environments is not a problem—it is a source of energy, learning, and creativity.
- Refrain from seeing people in a static way. People can—and do— change. (Constantly!)
- Unexpressed emotions are frequently misinterpreted. Lead by communicating feelings and by making sure people have an opportunity to express theirs.
- Tensions and challenges are expected among committed people. Acknowledge these tensions and address them as a priority. Do this directly—face-to-face if possible—with the person you are struggling with (rather than grumbling behind that person's back, or sending them an email).
- Use check-in rounds to build community. In restorative justice leader Kay Pranis's words, "people can be relaxed when they know they matter." Doing check-ins in a consistent rhythm, especially during stress or time crunches, conveys important values. While this can usually be done in a time-efficient manner, sometimes it cannot—and that's okay. (The power of check-in rounds cannot be overstated. Every person interviewed for this book named check-ins as a critical aspect of the Institute's culture.)
- Challenge and debate over ideas and strategies *strengthen* groups; unexpressed concerns do not.

---

87. Colleagues at BayNVC, especially Inbal and Miki Kashtan, helped me to learn and practice these concepts.

- Offer an assumption of innocence to colleagues when oversights occur (like forgetting to check a decision with you or dropping you from an email chain). Be slow to assume poor intentions.
- Rotate facilitation and leadership to nurture each person's understanding of group practices and to foster shared leadership.

In general, practice the basics around trust: be consistent, communicate clearly and as promptly as possible, and admit mistakes. Attention to trust works best when it's continuous, not occasional. Rhythms matter in groups and offer healing for challenges experienced at work, and at home. Benefits I observe include less stress in acknowledging errors and receiving support, swifter acknowledgement of tensions and misunderstandings, and far more laughter. All of that increases loyalty to one another, clear communication, and creativity, and decreases absenteeism and turnover.

In the very first workshop I ever did at the Institute, I couldn't believe how fast humans were able to build community. It really blew my mind. I came at a time I was feeling really despondent. I saw what was possible with a little bit of facilitation and an infused sense of respect and love. It refreshed my understanding and belief that we are really wired for this.

—Gwen, served as board member then staff at the M. K. Gandhi Institute

Your Turn: Think over a few of your closest professional relationships. How does trust factor in these connections? Are you able to creatively disagree, or do you keep quiet to maintain connection? What most supports your sense of trust in others? In yourself?

Chapter Seven Key Ideas
- Unresolved conflict impedes progress.
- Practice walking toward conflict in any way you can.
- Consider the conflict balance sheet—the benefits and the cost to avoiding a conflict versus attempting to resolve it. The costs of avoidance are often overlooked.
- Conflict can offer learning through reflection on our underlying beliefs about others and about conflict itself. Enhance learning by seeing the "other side" as human beings and potential teachers.

- When conflict occurs in high trust environments there is freedom to disagree, learn, and become more collectively creative.
- Structure, relationship, and skills are equally important for effective conflict processes.
- Dedicated spaces for conflict are supportive to groups in helping them normalize and even benefit from their differences of opinion and views.
- Trust is the single biggest asset in relationships and groups. Create, sustain, and re-establish trust as needed via consistency, clear communication, and freely acknowledging errors and misunderstanding (among other strategies).

Chapter Eight
Leadership—Embodied Nonviolence

What does it mean to be a leader? Your mind may leap to the image of a public figure standing at a podium speaking to a crowd, or a manager running a meeting. I believe a leader is more than that. In my view, leaders are people who decide to take responsibility for their actions, power, and position. This offers beautiful opportunities for embodying nonviolence.

Each of us has power in everyday ways, small and large. We see this power when workers organize for better wages. We see it in acts of kindness toward strangers and neighbors, in caring for Earth, in stepping up to resolve a conflict with friends or family. We see it when an administrator recognizes and overturns a discriminatory policy.

A leader is ...

... a bus driver who welcomes each passenger with a kind word.
... a produce manager at a grocery store who decides to buy from local farmers.
... a student who stops a friend from bullying.
... a manager who consistently honors every person on their team.
... a parent who disrupts harmful family patterns.

I invite you to notice and celebrate the leaders who quietly surround you every day.

Choosing Leaders

In 2017, I was in a little restaurant outside Syracuse, New York, having lunch and planning a workshop with my friend Cindy Squillace and Cindy's friend Freida Jacques, an Onondaga Nation clan mother.[88] We were setting up a visit for a group of University of Rochester undergraduates and their professor to the Skä•nonh Great Law of Peace Center. The center is on the edge of Onondaga Lake, a sacred place for the Haudenosaunee. It is the site where their confederacy was founded approximately 1,000 years ago. In the corner of the dim room, a television glowed and President Donald Trump was on the screen.

Freida glanced at the screen and said, "I'll never understand how you people choose your leaders." As a clan mother, Freida is one of the women responsible for choosing which men will serve as leaders for the Onondaga. She is also one of the people responsible, if leaders are not serving the people's interests, for removing them. Freida has been choosing leaders for years. She continued, "I look for leaders starting in childhood. I don't choose leaders who like to stand in front of the room and talk. I look for those who shovel driveways in the winter or who fill the woodbox without being asked."

This exchange reminded me of a similar one in 2002 at a board meeting for the Center for Nonviolent Communication (CNVC). During those weeklong meetings I was often restless, prowling around the room, half happy to be there and half impatient with the discussions. One day, while feeling especially impatient, I took an extended bathroom break. By the time I returned, they had nominated me for board chair! My grumpiness

---

88. The Onondaga Nation is one of the six nations that comprise the Haudenosaunee Confederacy. For more information, visit https://www.haudenosauneeconfederacy.com/.

escalated. A short while later, I was approached by Jorge Rubio Vollert, a Nonviolent Communication teacher from Colombia. At the time, he was the project manager of CNVC's efforts in South America. He urged me to say yes to the role, saying, "Only people who truly do not want power can be trusted with it." I took the role, with the group's understanding that I did not want to be board chair, but instead a board *couch*—making room for everyone to lead.

I've had the privilege of serving in several leadership positions, the privilege of hiring people, and the honor of being able to connect people to various opportunities. What I have learned from experiences like these is to look for people with certain qualities: an orientation toward service and to serving from love rather than from wanting to be loved.[89] I discern these qualities from noticing how an individual consistently treats others, their behavior in groups, and how they respond during stressful moments.

At the Gandhi Institute, we invited everyone to be involved in choosing new hires by expanding the interviewing team to include others beside myself and by making hiring decisions through consensus. In consultation with the board and colleagues, I chose to pass on my leadership role at the Gandhi Institute in 2021. The hiring process for the new person involved the board and staff who wanted to participate. As we reviewed the applicants, our focus included the values and internal practices of the individual, and how they would fit into the workplace culture we've been cultivating.

When staff have a voice in choosing their leadership, an organization becomes more of a self-sustaining ecosystem that does not rely on any individual—no matter their position—to flourish. This helps everyone to weather changes and struggles while upholding values and with respect for all. I feel joy and contentment watching the Institute thrive, even as it continues to change and struggle at times. Throughout my time there, I strove to make the Institute a self-sustaining ecosystem that did not rely upon me to flourish. Even during the immense pressures of the pandemic and its aftermath, the team is continuing to create an island of grounded hope.

Your Turn: How are staff and leaders chosen in the places where you work, worship, and volunteer? What do you look for in a leader? What leaders do you most admire, and why do you admire them? Who inspires you in the leadership roles you currently occupy?

---

89. The beautiful poem "Love" by Czesław Miłosz speaks to these themes.

Transparency

To be a transparent leader means to share good news and positive feedback, *and* to truthfully admit setbacks, errors, and shortcomings. Transparency cuts through suspicion, misdirection, and lies. It takes courage.

Transparency supports healthy relationships and leadership in a variety of ways. The practice of check-ins offers an opportunity to express with openness. It helps others know that it's safe to bring their whole selves into a meeting, project, or workplace. Transparency is key when addressing mistakes. When the person who makes the mistake honestly mourns their choices or limitations and invites others to name any impact, it opens space for deeper relationships and learning.

I have a longtime friend and collaborator with whom I have had dozens of meetings over the years. I look forward to our time together for the consistent combination of fun and productivity we generate. Recently I noticed that this person appeared to be irritated with me. Having noticed it, after receiving support, I practiced transparency and acknowledged my concern that something was off between us. Although it might feel easier to tell myself something like, "It's their problem, it's on them to reach out," I often initiate communication in situations like these.

Narratives about leadership are absorbed through numerous channels: school, media, our own experience. One such narrative is that leaders are confident and knowledgeable. I have found that this leads to deception as people occupying leadership roles try to cover their insecurity, or misrepresent choices rather than acknowledge errors. Instead of bluffing, try saying "I don't know" or "I'm not sure." As a leader, share stories about times you did the wrong thing for what, at the time, felt like the right reasons. Modeling relaxed self-acceptance is good medicine to be around and gives permission for others to be honest too.

Your turn: What are the spaces in your life where you feel able to express openly, and what benefits do you experience as a result? In what settings can you advocate for increased transparency through practices like check-ins and feedback?

You Can't Lead If You Don't Love

One of the amazing things about being human is that we find what we are looking for. When we look for hate, we find it. When we look for love, we find that. This crafts the lens that we have. The stories that we believe create our reality. If we're not terrified of one another, there's nothing that we can't do.
—Arno Michaelis

Where there is love, there is life.
—M. K. Gandhi

During a celebration of Dr. Martin Luther King Jr.'s birth and life, author and former PBS host Tavis Smiley said, "You can't lead if you don't love." While many of us understand the role of loving others, the inward direction of love—which generates transparency and self-acceptance—is often overlooked. Without cultivating this love, the self-judgments leak out, especially on those close to us.

In affirming self-love, I'm speaking of self-compassion, which might feel like indulgence.[90] Mercy and self-acceptance matter. The research says that our capacity for social critique and action are severely inhibited by self-judgment.[91] Learning to transform judgments of self and others into acceptance and love helps to prepare us for the hard work of becoming conscious stewards of our own power and privilege.

It takes work. All of us have received conditioning and patterns from our families and life experiences. Some patterns support well-being, others detract. In my family, judgments lead to unspoken resentment and severed connections. I watched these patterns ripple out from my parents' generation to my own generation and onto the next, causing rifts, pain, and lost opportunities for learning and healing.

The way I see it, transformation of judgments is an inside job—a part of healthy leadership that gives a sense of freedom, especially in that precious piece of real estate between our ears. It keeps us from walking around in a cloud of criticality. It helps restore a sense of focus, choice, and equanimity, and deepens understanding of our own operating instructions. Lastly, it aids in making fine-tuned adjustments so that

90. https://greatergood.berkeley.edu/article/item/the_five_myths_of_self_compassion
91. Michelle Fine, *Framing Dropouts: Notes on the Politics of an Urban Public High School,* 116.

we less frequently say and do things we regret. Taking responsibility for transforming judgments has wonderful side effects in friendships, marriage, and professional life.

I often hear feedback that I create an atmosphere of emotional safety for others. I believe this is largely due to this practice of transforming judgments of self and others.

Author David Foster Wallace sums up this orientation, describing creativity:

> It seems like the big distinction between good art and so-so art lies somewhere in the art's heart's purpose, the agenda of the consciousness behind the text. It's got something to do with love. With having the discipline to talk out of the part of yourself that can love instead of the part that just wants to be loved.

Nourishing the part of yourself that loves, and acting from that part, is a potent recipe for human endeavors: to create, speak, and lead from love.

Your turn: What helps you transform self-judgments? What needs do self-judgments serve for you? In which areas of your life do you act or lead from love?

Over-Functioning

Author Geri Scazerro defines over-functioning leadership as "Doing for others what they can and should do for themselves." Among other problems, over-functioning leadership is usually accompanied with a high emotional price tag. Not only is someone doing their job *and* yours, they may silently resent the dynamic even while participating in it.

When you find yourself over-functioning, try out one of these approaches to transform this sticky pattern:

- Include yourself in your own care. When you work extra days or hours, schedule time off for balance, and communicate about it to make sure colleagues see it in action.
- Learn to identify when you are over-functioning and instead make supportive space for someone else to step forward.

- Pay attention to needs you are trying to meet when you "save the day." What do you get out of this habit? When you have these answers, you can find other ways to address the situation.

Over-functioning leadership also undermines others. Leadership coach John Engels recommends that parents and managers refrain from offering "the support that stops development." People need space to grow, make mistakes, drop balls, and pick them up again.

Please don't interpret these words to mean that leaders ought not to offer advice or ideas. A significant aspect of leadership when responding to requests for help is asking questions and making suggestions. This approach is supported by a study on listening of 3,500 people that compared good listeners to trampolines: "They are someone you can bounce ideas off of—and rather than absorbing your ideas and energy, they amplify, energize, and clarify thinking. They make you feel better not merely passively absorbing, but by actively supporting. This lets you gain energy and height, just like someone jumping on a trampoline."[92]

To identify over-functioning, watch for sacrificial patterns in relation to others, to projects, or to areas of responsibility, then try to be both merciful *and* vigilant about changing those patterns. In recent years, I caught myself over-functioning in that classic activity for nonprofits: fundraising. Responsible for securing the financial resources for our organization, I was struggling, feeling unsuccessful and increasingly resentful. Instead of telling myself an old message like, "Tough, it's part of the job," I asked for more help from staff, volunteers, and board members. The benefits were tangible in terms of our budget, great professional development for team members, and for my internal landscape. Working with others on these projects increased creativity, learning, and inspiration. It decreased my stress and increased our overall functioning.

In my family, a current project where I find myself over-functioning is caring for my parents, especially my mom. I can do everything faster than she can, sometimes at great cost to both of us. When I'm doing almost everything for her, unless it's urgent, it's to meet my needs, or because I feel impatient. At my best, I give her space to struggle to stand, or reach something, or answer a question from a health care provider, rather than

---

92. Jack Zenger and Joseph Folkman, "What Great Listeners Actually Do," *Harvard Business Review* (July 2016). https://hbr.org/2016/07/what-great-listeners-actually-do.

doing it for her. She feels more empowered and appreciates my respect for her autonomy. Interrupting the power of over-functioning allows us to balance both of our needs. The same is true within leadership roles.

Your Turn: In what spaces and relationships would you describe yourself as over-functioning? What patterns and needs are in play when this happens? What is one relationship where it would help you and others to lean in and change that dynamic?

Earning Trust—and Being Worthy of It

Pay attention to signs that someone around you is feeling undervalued or has lost his or her self-confidence. Have that difficult conversation with the people around you to air out the issue. Because when you don't address insecurity, it's like the family secret that everyone knows but no one talks about.

—Tom and David Kelley

We perceive the world through the filter of our conditioning and experiences. This means that others see us through their assumptions and experiences about people of a similar age, race, and gender. In the workplace and in other groups, they will likely see us through the lens of previous encounters with colleagues, volunteers, and leaders. Rather than becoming defensive or indignant, we can relax and anticipate this dynamic as a normal one.

Be prepared to prove you are worthy of trust. If your race, ethnicity, class background, and age differ from your colleagues (which hopefully it will), the process of earning trust is likely to take longer. Relaxing with this process respects the lived experience and funds of knowledge of others, which usually include painful, unresolved experiences. The work of earning trust is an expression of cultural humility.

To accelerate the process, I recommend faithfully modeling trustworthy rituals and routines. Some examples that were already mentioned in the book include check-ins, structures of feedback, collaborative agenda setting, rotating facilitation, and including new people in that rotation as rapidly as possible.

Other practices for earning trust include:

- Monitoring when and how often you speak, and using as few words as possible
- Collaborative decision making
- Consistent use of feedback processes and implementing feedback
- Doing tasks like adding a chair for a new person, clearing away dishes, taking out the garbage, shoveling snow
- Volunteering to help with a project led by a team member, or being the one to take notes

Some of these suggestions can become part of a group or organizational culture. Others are personal practices that offer the chance to educate, embody, and serve, moment by moment. All of these practices are ground-work. The real test unfolds when you and another person have your first conflict. How well you handle that mutual growth opportunity helps to set the stage for the relationship going forward.

My recommended default setting: always act like people are watching.

Your Turn: Where are you seen as a leader? Are you able to retain self-awareness regarding your power in those spaces? If not, what support would enable you to become more conscious, more of the time?

Trouble in Paradox

The opposite of one profound truth may very well likely be another.
—Neils Bohrs

At the M. K. Gandhi Institute, you never feel too important and also you know you matter. I don't feel above anyone, I actually feel humbled in many situations. And I feel like I deeply belong. I don't need to bring much more than myself. I want more places like this to exist, in every neighborhood.
—Bianca, served as staff at the M. K. Gandhi Institute

I experience paradox as the hinge upon which human cultures—and souls—swing. A **paradox** is when two or more seemingly opposing realities coexist. We live, breathe, and exist in a state of paradox. To be human is to be alive with contradictions and seemingly opposing truths, an idea that both science[93] and many religious traditions uphold. As a leader who honors diverse perspectives and sees differences as a source of creativity, it's useful to name paradoxes at play, especially in conflict situations. Some familiar expressions of paradox include:

- Less is more.
- Damned if you do, damned if you don't.
- The beginning of the end.

Another example: each of us is unique *and* fundamentally the same. How do you resolve the question of your specialness? The exploration and the answers offer significant clarity.

If we believe we are special, we feel self-confident, able to pursue our dreams and to delight in our uniqueness. We remember that the great mystery of life expresses itself through us in a new and original way. We may have a strong sense of self-identity, offering us clarity and courage.

At the same time, if we believe we are special we may feel we deserve more. We are seduced by the notion that our individual or national or racial or religious or educational sense of specialness justifies higher rewards and greater access to opportunity or justice. Consciously or unconsciously, we make excuses for how inequalities tip in our favor. For instance, our local District Attorney was recently caught on camera by a police officer demanding to be let off for a speeding violation because of her importance.

On the other hand, even across the vast diversity of human beings, we have an incredible depth of similarity and common ground. Acknowledging commonalities unleashes potential. Transformative leaders make use of their own gifts by cultivating the ability to see themselves in others, in a meaningful recognition of shared humanity. As poet Maya Angelou put it, "we are more alike than we are different." In the shared terrain of what makes us human are laughter, tears, dreams, hopes, and fears. We want our children to be safe. We mourn when we lose our loved ones. This commonality is a window into our fellow human beings, and into other life forms as we begin to understand the relationships that animals and trees have with one another. It allows us to experience moral imagination, compassion, insight, and action.

93. https://youtu.be/jcOx77t9c2s

Disagreements and conflicts frequently contain paradoxes, both internal as well as interpersonal ones. We are taught to make instant judgments when we see contradictions, deciding right and wrong, good and bad. A powerful example of paradox is the misunderstanding about the phrase "Black lives matter." Is saying that Black lives matter implying that Black lives mean more, or that they need to mean more, or something else entirely? Awareness of paradox facilitates a shift to a bigger frame that supports inquiry and understanding for all—a key aspect of nonviolence.

People who see themselves in others often stand out for their humility, inclusivity, and graceful use of power. They may stand out because, as Howard Thurman said, "You cannot humiliate humility." Some particularly useful insights into humility and leadership derive from studying the impact of rank—a concept we will explore in the next section.

Your Turn: What are examples of paradoxes you notice? Do you enjoy that complexity, or struggle to find one right answer? Are there people you admire who seem able to hold opposing ideas in a healing way?

Understanding Rank

Effective interactors know how to cross thresholds of difference. One can deepen the practice of effective interactions by understanding and identifying key patterns of domination and liberation.
—Cyndi Suarez

There is no true peace possible for the man who still imagines that some accident of talent or grace or virtue segregates him from other men and places him above them.
—Thomas Merton

Earlier, I mentioned the importance of understanding our rank and privilege, and how useful that understanding can be. Among other insights, it can help us spot the discrepancies in our empathy toward others. In many ways, a working knowledge of rank offers a scenic overlook on the slippery slope of our biases.

Since I began working, even as a teenage volunteer, I have noticed a pattern: influential and well-intentioned people often seem unconscious of how they influence others through their status. When individuals are aware of their status, they sometimes feel paralyzed or guilty, and unable to see how they could use that status in a conscious, constructive way.

This shows up in a variety of settings: Managers downplay the power they hold in relation to staff. Big donors appear oblivious to the pressure organizations feel to look good. In one specific situation, a national organization (whose work inspires me greatly) had a founder whose unconsciousness regarding rank almost—and luckily did not—destroyed the organization. It did, however, require the use of precious resources of time and effort to address, taking energy away from their mission for months.

In 2003, I was invited to be a guest in a yearlong program for senior leaders in the World Bank. Leaders from around the world traveled for multiday retreats. It was a major investment of resources. To celebrate the program's conclusion months later, I attended an event in Washington, DC, at World Bank headquarters for a dinner celebration. It was meant to honor the learning and importance of the program. The person who was then head of the bank arrived with great fanfare to offer a few remarks to the hundreds of people gathered. During the Q&A, a participant asked a question that evidently provoked irritation, as he responded with contempt to the question. I felt the impact, a chill in the room. For me, that response unraveled the culture change the program had attempted to achieve.

I decided to send a letter to him. Among the hundreds of participants, I was one of the few not employed by the World Bank. I wrote what I'd observed, and expressed concern, especially as someone who had been invited because of my expertise in communication. In response, I received a form letter and a thick report celebrating the bank's work. While I would have valued hearing whether my letter had reached this leader and offered some (possibly rare) honest feedback, that wasn't the point. The point was to make use of my relative rank and privilege.

Early in my professional life, I saw the dynamics of unconscious use of rank and its adverse effects in other settings. My determination to avoid this dynamic led me to the work of Amy and Arnold Mindell. In one of their terrific books, *Sitting in the Fire*, the Mindells define **rank** as "the sum of all of our privileges." A **privilege** is a special advantage enjoyed by some, often at the exclusion or detriment of others. There are many kinds of privileges: race, gender, sexuality, education, wealth, religion, and more. As the Mindells note, many are inherited, not earned.[94]

Three ideas from the Mindells are particularly relevant to understanding our leadership styles. The first is the concept that rank and privilege are addictive—we want as much as we can get and are loath to relinquish it. This idea helps explain why those in power may end up abusing their status in an effort to hang on to it. This insight keeps the focus on the issue, rather than using time and emotional energy in outrage or disbelief at individual actors, or at the frequency of the pattern.

In many of its aspects power is like drugs: the need . . . is unknown to those who have not experienced them, but after the initiation, which may be accidental, addiction is born, dependency, and needs forever larger doses; also born is a rejection of reality and return to infantile dreams of omnipotence.

—Primo Levi

The second big idea is that, though all of us have some form of advantage, we tend to overlook or not recognize them. Instead, we identify with obstacles and privileges we do *not* have; we see ourselves through the lens of our subjugated identities. This cognitive bias has been colorfully labeled as "headwinds/tailwinds asymmetry."[95] Meanwhile, those around us see us in reverse: they see us through the lens of what we *do* have.

A third influential idea is that while many forms of privilege are inherited or fixed, others are fluid. Education, experience, skills, talents, longevity with an organization—all of these change over time. Some forms of rank are situational. What makes me high rank in many situations can make me low rank in others, and vice versa. The most painful example I can offer is the clear advantage of being white: surviving encounters with law enforcement, better outcomes in healthcare settings, opportunities to focus on my career rather than being expected to combat racism on top of doing my regular job. The "invisible knapsack" that antiracism educator Peggy McIntosh named years ago is jammed with privilege.[96] I have found that this can feel like low rank in community spaces with many People of the Global Majority where the distrust of white people means it can take a long time to build authentic connection. Or, it may not happen at all.

---

94. Arnold Mindell, *Sitting in the Fire: Large Group Transformation Using Conflict and Diversity,* 71-73.
95. https://everydaypsych.com/how-the-headwinds-tailwinds-asymmetry-shapes-your-thinking/
96. https://nationalseedproject.org/Key-SEED-Texts/white-privilege-unpacking-the-invisible-knapsack

The idea that rank is fluid and situational asks for a degree of responsibility that may feel challenging to consider. From sharing these ideas with many people over time, it seems most of us focus on the challenges that our life holds rather than the privileges, out of habit and perhaps at times to avoid contemplating our relation and responsibility to others. Saying this feels tricky because I am *not* trying to inspire guilt. Rarely does anyone make positive or permanent changes from guilt—resentment and lower trust are more likely outcomes. Positive regret, on the other hand, often accompanies learning and lasting change.

To illustrate some nuances of rank, here is a summary of my current rank profile. I update and refine this summary regularly, reflecting on what is changeable and what is not.

High Rank:

> Age: At 61, many leaders are my age and older. (Gandhi was 61 when he conceived of and led the Salt March!)
> Race: As a white person, here is a small example of the many benefits I receive: if I am given an award or asked to serve on a committee, I don't wonder if the invitation is race-related.
> Socioeconomic: I am middle class, a homeowner.
> Marital status: I am married.
> Parent: I am a mother of three.
> Sexual orientation: I am heterosexual
> Education: I hold bachelor's and master's degrees.
> Spiritual: I am a teacher, leader, and survivor of personal tragedy.
> Physical: I am generally healthy.
> Nationality: I am a citizen of the United States, where I live.
> Position/employment: I serve as an advisor/consultant in a variety of settings.
> Gender: I am cisgender.
> Neurotypical: For example, reading (a socially-approved form of learning) comes easy to me.

Above are the forms of advantage that offer privilege. Below is what makes me feel less privileged. Notice overlap between what offers high and low rank.

Low Rank:

> Age: At 61, I am not young, and sometimes feel people perceive me as less relevant.
>
> Socioeconomic status: Like other middle-class people, I have seen my real income shrink. Because of years in low-paid nonprofit positions, I have small retirement savings compared to people who worked in the public or for-profit sectors.
>
> Gender: Like other white women, I will average 80 percent of the salary of a male with my same qualifications. If I were a woman of color facing the intersection of race and gender, that percentage overall is closer to 65 percent.[97]
>
> Education: I do not have a PhD and work in academia where that is an issue.
>
> Technology: I don't enjoy using technology.
>
> Parent: One of my children is no longer alive.
>
> Physical: I am overweight.
>
> Nationality: While there are many advantages to being a citizen of the United States, in many places outside the US, that is a liability. In many places I have visited, the United States is seen as a purveyor of violence and greed.
>
> Position: I surrendered the title, position, and prestige of being an executive director. I do, however, retain some rank based on being emeritus director.

I perpetually seek to identify new forms of privilege. A recent addition to my list: unlike people around the world whose childhood homes and neighborhoods have been destroyed by war, climate disruption, or gentrification, I can still visit my childhood neighborhood and recognize it.

Sometimes, we notice privilege after temporarily or permanently losing some aspect of it. I recommend exploring your profile, to examine your identity in all of its complexity and intersections. This will also offer increased awareness of how others perceive you, grounding in difficult moments, and hopefully eagerness to lessen your impact on others—all of which can be a significant benefit to healthy leadership. In the next chapter we'll learn to see systems of all kinds, including those that generate advantage and privilege.

---

97. https://www.forbes.com/advisor/business/gender-pay-gap-statistics/

During the World Bank gatherings, I had numerous opportunities to interact one-on-one with highly-placed people, and heard repeated expressions of powerlessness. Despite occupying high rank in that powerful institution, they believed that they did not ultimately have much power. Similar expressions from highly-placed people in other settings have become all too familiar. Especially from these opportunities, I have come to believe that identifying and using our rank as a resource offers significant transformational potential for all people.

Here is one example of how I used my rank: Over many months, I attended diversity roundtable meetings at a local university. These involved many Global Majority students and colleagues, as well as numerous white people. The room where we met was adorned with photos of former students from the early to mid-twentieth century. The people in these images were 100 percent white and 100 percent male. I started to ask around about changing venues—then had a better idea. Using my rank as a director of an affiliated nonprofit, and less at risk of being caught up in campus politics, I approached the dean of that college and pointed out the incongruence of the art, requesting her help to make it a space that welcomes all people. That conversation led to an overhaul of art throughout that part of campus and created a friendship that continues today.

Awareness and mindful use of rank is an opportunity, and also a responsibility. Lack of awareness of status, rank, and privilege affects our ability to live nonviolently. It collectively blinds us to our role in maintaining structural and systemic violence. It masks how we may benefit from these structures even as we oppose them, which prevents us from working towards meaningful change. When it feels difficult to see, ask "Who is benefiting from the current structures? Who is not benefitting?"

Your turn: Think of a time when you were able to advocate for yourself or for another. What forms of rank supported that effort? Take time to review the forms of privilege and rank you do and do not have. What surprises you, and what is uncomfortable to notice?

Preventing Harm

Using rank with all the courage and creativity we can muster is a nonviolent practice. Gandhi spoke of this as "trusteeship" of the gifts we receive in life, earned and unearned. Here's one story of an attempt to be responsive and accountable with those gifts.

One summer, I heard from a Black community leader about a pro-police march being organized by a local radio host. The route would go through neighborhoods in Rochester with an intensive historic concentration of over-policing and poverty. In 1964, parts of the neighborhood had exploded in what Black residents called resistance and in what white residents called a riot. This Black leader predicted a high likelihood of violence if the march were to take place.

I had been studying Kingian Nonviolence[98] and knew that one of the first steps in the Kingian approach is research. I asked an intern to find out everything they could about this talk show host. Meanwhile, I began reaching out to the most influential white organizational and business leaders I knew, asking them to contact the station manager and tell them that their advertising dollars were not going to go to stations that fomented violence. (This choice to mobilize white leaders was strategic; I guessed that Black leaders calling the station might fuel more rhetoric.) The intern discovered that this talk show host was Mormon—vital information, as I knew that the Mormon Church was trying to clean up its historic act in terms of racism. I reached out to a former colleague who was then a bishop in the Mormon Church. He agreed to talk to the radio host, and I offered to speak with him as well, on-air or off-air. Between these efforts, and the efforts of others, the march was canceled.

When you are going to move to action, think carefully about strategy. Use observation and ask for concrete feedback. Will the proposed action do more harm than good? Kingian Nonviolence principles, and the observation practice in Nonviolent Communication, support constructive responses to move care and concern into learning-filled action.

Life is mysterious. Sometimes we can prevent harm and do remarkable good by being accountable for our values regardless of circumstance. This was the case with Nelson Mandela, who studied white South Africans' language and history while imprisoned without hope of release for twenty-eight years. Like other Black South Africans, he received brutal treatment and discrimination from white Afrikaners. Mandela did not study Afrikaans culture and language from a psychic sense that he would

---

98. https://thekingcenter.org/about-tkc/the-king-philosophy/

someday be president, or even be released from prison. He studied because he didn't want to lose himself to bitterness and hate. Very unexpectedly, the knowledge and perspective he gained over those years informed his ability to understand and relate to Afrikaner leaders and people. It was foundational in helping to create the miraculous transition of society and government as apartheid was dismantled.

Your Turn: Think of a time when something was happening in a group or the broader community, and you felt called or inspired to help. What happened? What did you learn? What do you wish you had known to do differently? Gather a group and share these questions with them. What patterns do you notice in the group's responses?

Double Signals[99]

An Irish friend once told me that Irish people, like other colonized peoples, "speak out of both sides of their mouths." She was referencing a cultural legacy of speaking indirectly or even in doublespeak because it was not safe to do otherwise. Any individual from a group that has been or is oppressed may resort to double signals without conscious awareness. It can be a reflex to create safety or autonomy. In US culture, I find that fear of conflict and a driving need for inclusion lead many people to say things they don't mean. The presence of these "double signals" means that the expiration date on any agreement we make may be even sooner.

Double signals are important to notice when a power differential exists— as between parent and child, or between staff member and manager—or when there is tension in a relationship or group. Since most relationships, even friendships, come with subtle power differences, life offers lots of practice in spotting these. Discomfort and truth often hover just below the surface of the double signal. Bringing it to light can be a relief and sometimes a revelation. Any communication benefits from the practice of noticing and naming double signals.

Sarcasm is a familiar double signal—a way of blowing off steam and of signaling unhappiness. In a conflict-averse relationship, group, or society, it's a strategy that has its uses. I grew up around sarcasm and used to be sarcastic regularly. However, from seeing the confused looks on my

---

99. Double signals are another dynamic named by the Mindells.

children's faces when they heard it from me, I came to think of sarcasm as a form of low-level dishonesty. Noticing that, my husband and I decided to minimize sarcasm toward each other and toward our kids. It was a good move. Sarcasm from leaders can be similarly hurtful. When I revert to sarcasm, it's a signal that my energy and emotional resources are low.

Organizations, businesses and groups routinely send double signals. Most of us have experienced the gap between policy and practice, between stated values of care and the lived reality. That gap generates confusion and cynicism, which is corrosive to purpose and effectiveness. It is relieving and empowering to name that dynamic in organizational life as a source of pain and as a place for potential improvement.

One barrier to acknowledging the gap is the difficulty of acknowledging harms, past and present. While accountability might feel overwhelming to contemplate, it can be faced. Both symbolic reparations—apologies, memorials, or commemorations—and material reparations can mend the gap and begin to align organizational actions with values.

The approaches described in these pages are intended to shrink that gap while remembering that no single person is to blame and to remember that all groups struggle with some version of this. We can roll up our sleeves and put our effort into building cultures where we name that gap between stated values and lived reality, and work to continuously narrow it.

Your turn: Can you think of double signals you routinely send, or receive? What about double signals of organizations where you work, worship, and volunteer? Are there opportunities for accountability that could help shrink the gap between stated values and actions?

Chapter Eight Key Ideas

- Leaders are people who take responsibility for their actions, power, and position.
- Choose leaders by ensuring everyone has a voice in the process. Look for those who serve from love rather than wanting to be loved.
- Build transparency with check-ins and being swift to admit mistakes and limits of knowledge.

- Transforming judgments of self and others helps us to lead and serve from a place of love.
- Over-functioning leads to burnout and undermining others. Learn to balance your needs and others' by asking for help and respecting their autonomy.
- Leaders are naturally viewed through others' previous experiences. Personal practices and group norms offer opportunities to build trust.
- Conflicts often contain paradoxes. Identifying them creates space to understand everyone involved rather than making instant judgments.
- Build awareness and understanding of rank and privilege to prevent unconscious harm and create opportunities to use them to benefit everyone.
- Accountability for the gifts of rank and privilege is a powerful practice.
- Look for double signals and bring them to light to shrink the gap between values and experience. Start looking for them in yourself, first.

Chapter Nine

Convergence: Living Systems & Nonviolence

Learning to See Living Systems

We don't see the world as it is, we see it as we are.

—Anaïs Nin

When I first visited the Institute in 2013, I learned about the systemic nature of violence and nonviolence. Since violence is systemic, nonviolence needs to be as well. Systemic thinking was throughout the work.

—Thomas, served as board member at the M. K. Gandhi Institute

Living systems are self-organizing life forms that interact with their environment. They are "open" systems, meaning that they affect and are affected by what is happening around them. Self-organizing means they operate without external oversight. For example, healthy natural systems, like a pond or a forest, don't need a manager or strategic plan to thrive. Self-organizing systems range in size from cells to galaxies. Ant and bee colonies are examples of living systems, as are our bodies and our organizations.

Sometimes when I talk about systems, I notice people's eyes glaze over a bit—it feels vague, intellectual, or overwhelming. And yet, we can learn to see ecosystems, economies, and human beings as living systems which have so much to teach us about how to make our work—and world—more nonviolent. Bringing a systems lens to daily life and work upholds values of seeking to understand rather than blame, of humility, and of honoring interconnectedness. Interconnection appears to be the binding principle of life in our amazing, unique planetary home.[100]

Remembering to employ a systemic lens helps to:

- Identify new allies and collaborators in the local community.
- Ride the waves of change rather than drowning in them.
- Know when to push forward with an effort and when to let it rest.
- Embrace the whirlwind of ideas—often conflicting—to identify solutions.
- Relax more and more with complexity, pushback, and conflict.
- Experience others as parts of a larger ecosystem, rather than as competitors.

Seeing in systems brings insight, focus, and equanimity to leadership roles and organizational life. The practices we have discussed—experimentation and tolerance for mistakes, the discipline of observations, holding spaces for multiple truths, and seeking feedback—all derive from attempting to see systems.

Grief work, solo and in community, is deeply entwined in seeing systems. Watching human-made systems at work can break our hearts. Noticing natural systems at work, like trees leafing out in spring and the miraculous migration of birds, inspires a sense of well-being. However, witnessing them unravel as part of climate change requires us to care for our mental and spiritual well-being.

---

100. I began learning to recognize systems at work through Joanna Macy's teachings, by studying permaculture, and by learning from indigenous authors and community members.

Energy—physical, mental and emotional— is the currency of systems. Principles of nonviolence powerfully shape how individual and combined energy is utilized, offering opportunities for nonviolent values and action to have an outsized influence. This is possible even as a solo actor, especially when we begin to embrace Paul Chappell's[101] assertion that "challenge is an acquired taste." If we have acquired a taste for challenge in *any* area of life, we can transport that mindset and behavior into other parts of our lives. When we combine with others the effect multiplies, powerfully.

In the 1990s, a new module was added to the fourth grade science curriculum. It taught every schoolchild in the United States about ecosystems. They study the web of life and how plants, animals, insects, rivers, weather, mountains, and so forth are all connected. The significance of this was—and is—profound. Perhaps it is one of the most foundational ways that our culture offers for teaching children how to "see" living systems.

Some people I spend time with were not taught to recognize systems, at work or elsewhere. The lens of individualism makes it difficult to "see" the internal system of our conditioning as well as external living systems in action.

One of my most useful insights from studying these ideas is to remember that systems live *inside and outside* us.[102] Even if we could snap our fingers and create an ideal world, we would end up replicating the patterns we are trying to escape. There are many examples of political upheaval when reformers attain office and end up replicating the dynamics and harms of those they struggled and suffered to replace. The necessity of working to change our internalized systems is a major driver for me in studying and advocating for principled nonviolence, rather than strategic nonviolence.

Once we learn to recognize and appreciate living systems, a question naturally arises on how to interact skillfully in ways that increase benefits and prevent harms. Whether the system you are contemplating is your family, your workplace, or community, the problem-solving approach many of us learned needs to be broadened. Philosopher Karl Popper suggests we look at problems as either clocks or clouds. A clock is something you can take to pieces, analyze the parts and see how it works. A cloud is a

---

101. Paul is a former US Army officer and current powerful peace educator. Find more about him and his organization at https://www.peaceliteracy.org/.
102. The "Habits of A Systems Thinker" cards from Thinking Tools Studio are a great online resource for learning to recognize systems. Find them at https://thinkingtoolsstudio.waterscenterst.org/cards.

dynamic system—you can't take it apart. The way to understand a cloud is to study it in a holistic way.[103] (And admire their beauty.)

Groups are pulled between these two models. They're *trying* to be clockwork machines, but they're *actually* living systems. When we try to treat any living system like a mechanical object, it rarely works well. Think about humans, or our Earth.[104] The rest of this chapter offers concrete approaches for applying systems thinking to our lives and work.

Your Turn: What living systems do you notice? Whatever you regularly complain and worry about is a good place to start looking. Most of us were taught to think that the places we work, worship, and volunteer operate like clocks, or assembly lines. Think about it: does that metaphor for group life relate to your lived experiences?

Relaxing with Complexity

Nothing is prescribed. Whatever happens is a direct result of everyone's input in meetings and events. It's like jazz—responding to whatever is there. We make music together. I feel like that will always end in people learning more.

—Joel, served as board member at the M. K. Gandhi Institute

Interconnectedness—within and between living systems—results in abundant complexity. It's what makes curry so flavorful, and some songs so great to dance to. It's also why some disputes are harder to resolve than others, or why working for change can be tricky. There are layers, myriad perspectives, and multiple, seemingly opposing, truths. Complexity ripples through human groups. It may reveal itself as a conflict, hurt feelings, or a sense of dread that we aren't in control. It can reveal itself in amazement and joy too.

One approach to managing this complexity is learning to notice and relax with it instead of trying to simplify situations to make them more comfortable. For instance, instead of using subtle force to streamline a situation according to my preference, I ask colleagues to arrange the workflow to suit their needs. Rather than keeping a meeting to a few

---

103. https://www.theatlantic.com/daily-dish/archive/2010/06/clouds-not-clocks/185941/
104. *The Secret Wisdom of Nature: Trees, Animals, and the Extraordinary Balance of All Living Things—Stories from Science and Observation* by Peter Wohlleben is filled with teaching stories on natural systems and surprising connections.

stakeholders, invite more people into the conversation. When a conflict arises, ride its waves rather than rush for resolution.

This is important because forcing complexity into false simplicity doesn't work. As the amazing Victor Lewis says, "Simple answers to complex problems tend to make problems worse."

Inspired by the work of author Amanda Ripley, the Solutions Journalism Project trained journalists in how to "complicate the narrative." Instead of one-sided stories, or the binary frameworks of *us vs. them* common in so many news stories, they encouraged reporters to bring up the many-faceted angles on an issue. For example, instead of framing the climate crisis as a battle between earth-lovers and fossil fuel companies, journalists can write about conservative families struggling to pay fuel bills and the need for better insulation programs. They can explore the struggles of local solar companies and other alternative energy initiatives. They can dig into the existential dread felt by young people and increasing suicide rates related to climate collapse. Complexity in news stories reflects lived realities. It gives language and information for navigating our times.[105]

Like many of us, my background and conditioning make it difficult to look through a systems lens consistently. I was taught to prefer simple clear answers rather than cultivating the capacity to relax with complexity. People like me, those from a dominant culture group and from a middle-class background, tend not to be accustomed to dealing with complexity. Society is designed to align with our expectations; we expect and even believe we deserve simple and easy answers. In addition, our culture enshrines monocrop thinking: silver-bullet solutions, one-size-fits-all, my way or the highway. . . You probably recognize this pattern. Relaxing with complexity is yet another opportunity to practice cultural humility.

Complexity enjoys having time to express itself. Our dominant paradigm perpetuates because we don't allow time to explore new or different ideas. Feeling short on time, we go with the familiar—or rather, the familiar to the dominant culture. Groups run into problems because they don't believe they have the time needed to foster relationships and increase participation in decision making. Or, the effort to change appears overwhelming. Think about city councils that use Robert's Rules

---

105. Check out these questions to complicate the narrative from Solutions Journalism: https://s3.amazonaws.com/sjn-static/CTN_Interview_Qs.pdf.

of Order[106] versus a talking circle: one method centers on getting to a solution, while the other centers on honoring every voice.

The people in our lives can help us learn to love complexity, especially those who walk with complex identities. One such friend for me is Rashid Muhammed, a Black father, husband, former Air Force officer, and former Gandhi Institute board member. We met in 2009 while sharing a tiny office at the University of Rochester. He then served as Muslim chaplain on campus and I was just starting at the Gandhi Institute, which was located on campus then. Rashid gifts me, and many others, with love and learning: about the beauty of Islam, the dynamics of oppression, and about music—especially jazz—as an art form of complexity, and of resistance. We spent hours one day listening to the rapid construction and deconstruction of themes within songs like Coltrane's "Chim Chim Cheree" (from *Mary Poppins*), and the commentaries Black artists like Coltrane were making to white culture via jazz.

One strategy for relaxing with complexity is to slow things down, to reduce overwhelm or anxiety, and to name the issues or factors in the situation. Whether leading, coaching, or facilitating, modeling is the most effective teaching I know. I often share what is authentic for me, expressing disappointment, sadness, or curiosity as they arise. Reacting with inquiry and openness when circumstances change speaks loudly. Mourning out loud when the change represents a sense of loss offers permission for others to name reactions and helps to clear a space to then collaboratively relate to the new circumstances.

Noticing, naming, and acting from the awareness of complexity is a critical mindset to cultivate. One practice that helps me to appreciate and engage with complexity is called stacking function, an idea that comes from permaculture. We'll take a look at this in the next section.

Your turn: What helps you to enjoy complexity—gardening, the dynamics of a sports team, music, artistic endeavors? Who helps you notice complexity with appreciation? When complexity inspires anxiety, what helps to ground you?

---

106. Robert's Rules of Order is a parliamentary procedure for meetings used in many US companies and governance structures.

Permaculture Principles

If we surrendered
to earth's intelligence
we could rise up rooted, like trees.

—Rainer Maria Rilke

In 2009, my husband David and I studied a discipline called permaculture. **Permaculture** is a creative design process based on whole-systems thinking, informed by ethics and design principles. This approach guides us to mimic the patterns and relationships in nature that can be applied to all aspects of human endeavor, from agriculture to ecological building, from appropriate technology to education and economics. While permaculture was originally focused on ecology and landscape design, I was intrigued by the overlap with nonviolence, from broad principles of honoring all life to specific practices like starting with slowing down and observing what is, rather than springing into action. Over time, these ideas have come to serve as a personal framework for designing projects and workspaces. They inform how I work, from management to facilitation to conflict transformation.

One permaculture principle to practice complexity is "stacking function." Stacking function is creating an element, plan, or project that can do many things at once. For instance, the right tree in a permaculture design can provide food, shade, building material, firewood, oxygen, animal habitat, and erosion prevention.

Trees and plants that are native to environments have evolved to participate in hundreds of beneficial relationships, whereas plant life introduced into an environment even a century before may have only had time to develop a scant handful. Applying this principle to human activity might hint at why long-term, community-based projects can generate more benefits—especially over time—than interventions from "outsiders."

In the academic discipline of systems thinking, I also hear stacking functions described as multisolving. Examples include: "an opportunity to solve two or more problems with the same budget, with the same effort and time. An opportunity to widen the circle of people who are going to show up and use their political power and their voices to create change."[107]

107. Check out the Multisolving Institute at https://www.multisolving.org/.

Workplaces can thoughtfully apply this concept of stacking function to support greater outcomes, staff satisfaction, and sustainability, from how we plan a project to how we assess its completion. For example, when the Gandhi Institute hosted its first webinar years ago, we noticed that it educated people outside our geographic area, helped staff to reflect on their work, and generated income. In addition, we conveyed an educational approach through how we organized the event, passing on models of collaboration, trust, and resource-sharing. The gardens at the Gandhi Institute, the school-based programming, youth grants, and other activities were developed with this lens.

Most decisions benefit from awareness of stacking function, from where we spend and store resources of every kind, to decisions about time use. For instance, especially due to climate impacts, I have chosen not to travel by air unless I have a stacking function of three or more reasons. Many trips have not happened as a result.

Stacking functions reframe complexity as a field of productive possibility and supports conservation of energy and resources. Thinking through this lens can be fun, like solving a puzzle.

Your turn: Where do you employ the idea of stacking function where you work, worship, and volunteer? What effort could benefit from bringing this perspective more consistently?

Harnessing the Power of Edges

No matter how good you think you are as a leader, my goodness, the people around you will have all kinds of ideas for how you can get better.
—Jim Yong Kim

Another relevant permaculture principle is "edge effect," also known as ecotones. It arises from scientific observations that a high degree of diversity naturally occurs where differences meet. This includes where fields meet forest, where you'll find a wide range of plants; or where shallow meets deep waters, where you will see a higher number of fish and aquatic species. The surface of the earth (where humans and so many other life forms live) is an edge between the planet and the atmosphere. Naturally occuring edges are fertile, diverse, and full of potential for growth and evolution.

Edges are everywhere, when you look for them. Even as I write these words, I notice that my morning quiet time takes place in the liminal, border space of my porch. Later, as I walk our dog, Tashi (my closest friend from another species), we meander through a grove of old oaks in the middle of the city. It is a place of juxtaposition, urban and natural, forested and residential. I finish my quiet time there after giving thanks to the trees for the gifts of breath and air.

Groups that contain many human edges—age, class, sexual orientation, religion, race, educational attainment, gender, and nationality, among others—are reliably the most inspiring spaces to spend time. Divergences of perspective, ideas, and approaches can be highly generative edges, keeping viewpoints from solidifying and cultivating flexibility in thought, reaction, and creativity. I believe groups like this may have the best chance of creating the emergence of the Beloved Community.

Working with edges requires awareness, and to know enough of our own operating instructions to prioritize partnering with others who complement rather than replicate them. The same goes for skills, talents, habits, weaknesses, patterns, worldviews, perspectives, and life experiences. Some questions to consider, to assess your operating instructions:

- Are you swift to speak, or slow?
- Are you a details-lover, or fine with saying, "That's good enough"?
- Do you enjoy infusing artistry into details, or are you more excited about efficiency?
- Do you like solo projects, or group endeavors?
- Are you comfortable in the spotlight, or are you happier behind the scenes?
- What are your strengths: writing, facilitating groups, crunching numbers, making sales, creating visual displays?
- What are your aversions: spreadsheets, graphic design, fundraising?

Whatever bouquet of gifts you bring, look for colleagues whose gifts differ from yours. Seek variety in age, race, religion, and cultural backgrounds. Move toward people who look at the world differently than you, who approach problems from another angle, and whose life experiences are dissimilar to yours.

To receive the most benefits from working with these diverse groups, here are three guidelines:

- Know that your perspective contains only a small fraction of the truth.
- Take the strong desire to be right as a sign of low internal resilience. Consider the question, "Do you want to be right or do you want to be effective?"[108]
- Expect to screw up or get things wrong sometimes, and know that others do too. When you do, prioritize making amends swiftly.

Your Turn: Reflect on some of your generative partnerships at work, past and present. Where do you differ from each other? What helps you successfully navigate your "edges" with others?

Feedback as a Gift

Something I saw modeled was asking for feedback consistently. That was something I loved, that it was woven into what it means to lead something.
—Jamie, served as staff at the M. K. Gandhi Institute

People need to be wrong as fast as they can.
—Andrew Stanton

Feedback reminds us that we matter, that our choices and endeavors and passions and lives count. It is critical for helping us to navigate groups, teams, and spaces with lots of generative edges. Feedback processes help to ameliorate conflict aversion. As discussed earlier, leaders like Gandhi and practices like permaculture and Nonviolent Communication stress the discipline of observation—to look carefully, to share and seek ongoing feedback.

When someone has the courage to tell us that something we have done has *not* worked for them, appreciate them. All of us have the choice to refrain from speaking the truth to each other. If someone offers you or your group a difficult truth or challenging message, choose to receive it as a gift—like the gift your nervous system offers when your hand holds an extremely hot object. Though painful, this information tells you to drop it before the pain gets worse.

---

108. Gratitude to my friend Maisha Enaharo for that question!

Appreciation will likely not be the very first response. It is normal to feel disappointed or distressed to hear when something—a project, or a message, or a conversation—has fallen short. However, as quickly as possible, shift to focusing on and expressing gratitude for the care and the courage it took to express a truth and for the learning that reliably follows. Often the learning is mutual. The more we practice with this perspective, the easier it becomes, and the more we benefit from the resulting strengthened relationships.

Asking for feedback at the conclusion of an effort, whether it be a talk, training, or conversation, is a great gift. You may hear that your efforts mattered more than you thought. You may get information about focus for the next time, and give your nervous system a chance to settle down before shifting to the next event in a crowded calendar. Feedback offered as part of the conclusion of a group offers a good review, as participants hear one another reflect on their "golden nuggets" from time spent together.

If you feel shy about asking for feedback, become devoted to offering it for a while and see what happens. Most of us do not know how much we matter to others, with the understandable and sometimes tragic corollary that we therefore do not understand how much our words and actions matter. Making sure the people around you *know* that they matter is a joyful discipline.

Incorporating feedback into group rhythms offers large returns. One way we worked to build a culture of continuous feedback at the Gandhi Institute was to conclude staff and board meetings, as well as any other meeting or training, with a few minutes dedicated to a process called "Pluses, Deltas, and Bright Ideas." At the conclusion of gatherings, we collect *pluses* (what worked well), *deltas* (how it could have worked better), and *bright ideas* (any relevant creative thought). Participating in this process multiple times each week creates a culture where speaking up is rewarded, and where learning and process are prioritized. The discipline of feedback helps transition with more wholeheartedness from one activity to another, especially if something has not gone as planned. This allows us to have closure about the experience and prevent our mental landscape from getting cluttered.

Creating a structured feedback process that participants engage in and continuously update helps incorporate the values of the organization. Ours included those expressed in the Gandhi Institute's staff commitments (see page 175). The process could include feedback about contributions, and opportunities for improvement and for clearing the air of lingering issues.

Many Gandhi Institute staff members interviewed for this book expressed how much these explicit processes help them to feel safe to experiment, since mistakes and "getting it wrong" are normalized. Reducing our conditioned fear of mistakes helps groups working on "cloud" issues—like organizational change or social issues—to succeed by failing faster and growing stronger from the experience.[109]

A special rhythm of feedback for Gandhi Institute staff are birthday circles. When someone has a birthday, part of the staff meeting is a circle of appreciation. Everyone speaks, sharing stories, concrete observations, and positive impacts of knowing that person. The birthday person is asked to offer appreciation for themselves. While new staff often joke about how nerve wracking it can be to participate and especially to appreciate themselves for the first time, it is a meaningful ritual. Some staff bring this practice to their family and friend gatherings.

Your Turn: Think of a time when you have offered and/or received feedback that stands out as impactful. What happened to make those experiences possible? How can you build ongoing feedback into your regular schedule? When and how often are team members meaningfully appreciated?

Collaboration

Let's hook up these minorities and make one hell of a majority.
—Fannie Lou Hamer

Greed starts out with spoiling relationships—we are always competing. If someone is going ahead of us, we want to bring them down.
—Arun Gandhi

Evolutionary biology demonstrates the power of cooperation between animals, plants, and ecosystems. Different forms of life offer a dazzling array of strategies to exchange resources and nourishment, from chemical

---

109. For more information on this approach, see Peter Manzo's article, "Fail Faster, Succeed Sooner," found here: https://ssir.org/articles/entry/fail_faster_succeed_sooner.

exchanges via air and soil to locomotion. These interactions increase resilience, foster adaptation, and essentially make all of life possible. This wonderful, endless exchange is inherent in our lovely planet's natural systems, and is different from the way many humans are educated to think and act.

In schools and organizations, we are taught to compete. This way of thinking teaches us to retain rather than exchange knowledge and resources. We do not learn to see, remember, or cherish connectedness. Collaboration is viewed as helpful by some, not as essential by all. The truth is that—especially for those of us trying to create significant and lasting change to social structures—collaboration is the only way to succeed. In the particular case of the Gandhi Institute: even if the Institute were 100 times, or 1000 times bigger, structural expressions of violence and their consequences are so entrenched that no one organization can possibly deal with them all. This is true in many spaces where we work, worship, and volunteer.

Urging collaboration between organizations, as well as within organizations, is not a new idea. But because of what we learn, excavating competition from our way of thinking and acting and instead enacting wholehearted collaboration is far more difficult. Here are some guidelines to unlearn competition and nourish a healthy ecosystem of collaborative growth:

- Define the network of organizations that comprise your community. Knowing it's potentially endless, map what makes sense. It can be geographic, practice-based, or defined by other criteria. It may include vendors, suppliers, funders, neighbors, clients, customers, or patients.
- Celebrate your community's achievements. Uplift their good work, talk about it, participate in it.
- Actively seek ways to share resources and work together.
- Hold regular check-ins to connect, celebrate, and seek ways to support one another.
- Pay attention when new projects are proposed within your organization. How will this affect others' work in that community?

Every organization can benefit—and offer benefits—by working closely with our defined community groups, as well as area colleges, banks, police, courts, activists, school systems, and religious communities. The competition mentality is an ingrained mindset, another piece of cultural conditioning we do not choose to receive. Shifting it requires dedicated effort.

Mudita is a practice from Buddhism of cultivating "sympathetic joy" at the success and good fortune of others.[110] When envy or jealousy arises in response to the good fortune of others, let that wave pass over you and consciously choose celebration. This practice helps to disable a competitive mindset. Over time, it rewires our responses and changes the norms of the culture we're building.

Feeling happy about, not threatened by, the opportunities and successes of other organizations and groups, including their individual leaders, has numerous good outcomes. (There's that stacking function, again!) It creates space for wholeheartedness, synergy, collaboration, and trust. For example, a few years ago, I received a call from a community partner, the director of a Rochester youth organization. They were scheduled to appear on a radio program and a member of their team had to cancel at the last minute. Would I join the interview? I agreed and as I introduced myself on the air, I explained that although I served as director of the Gandhi Institute, I had joined the show as a devoted fan of and donor to this other organization. The talk radio host was surprised that I was there to promote another organization. I cherish knowing that the director of this organization trusted me to show up for them that day.[111]

The repercussions of operating without collaboration became clear to me during my time with the Center for Nonviolent Communication (CNVC). While serving as a board member and later as board president (2001–2004), I saw painful, expensive patterns of competition between individuals teaching Nonviolent Communication. It was a wonderful teaching about walking toward conflicts and about the power of conditioning despite individual values and practices. The dynamic was so entrenched, we could not shift it. Instead, I studied it, hoping to avoid repetition.

That chance came when I served as Director/Celebrator at Bay Area Nonviolent Communication in Oakland, California, from 2004 to 2009. We set up a collaborative trainers model to establish ongoing connections and collaboration for regional trainers, and support for conflicts. Replacing the competition model with a collaborative focus helped us to become the largest regional group in the world sharing Nonviolent Communication at the time. It helped us move with more integrity as we shared the mindset and practices of Nonviolent Communication with thousands of individuals in that socially-conscious, influential part of the planet.

110. I feel grateful to have learned about mudita from Joanna Macy.
111. For another example of collaboration, read about Nonviolence Now on page 172.

Similarly, during my first years at the Gandhi Institute, we helped to create a collaborative called "Restorative Rochester" to enable all groups and individuals who were interested in restorative justice and restorative practices to work together and set collective goals. As a result, the Gandhi Institute rarely offered training for restorative work, as one of our community partners was already dedicated to that. Instead, we focused on accelerating the adoption of restorative practices regionally. Among other efforts, we did this by working with community partners to host films, by offering talks to dozens of groups on the social and financial benefits of restorative work, by organizing two conferences at Rochester City Hall, through media appearances, and by supporting restorative justice projects in schools and local courts. My favorite Restorative Rochester project was creating a newspaper that was dated from ten years in the future, an "imagineering" exercise. This realistic-looking piece helped people reimagine our community through the restorative lens—a very different way of understanding relationships and of addressing harm. I also helped other groups secure funding for their efforts.

Examples of collaboration—and its benefits—abound in my experience. They have given me and others uncountable gifts, supported exciting projects, and fostered wonderful relationships.

Your Turn: Think about the best collaboration you have experienced. What were the tangible benefits? What did you learn? What prevents you from collaborating in specific places or projects? What support could you use to shift into more collaborative ways of thinking, being, and doing in those spaces?

Get Well-Connected

To go big, stay small and get well connected.
—David Loy

I can't talk about the culture without talking about the physical presence of the house. That place is imbued with the feeling of the culture. Someone could walk in even if no one else was there and feel this is a place of peace, and of community.
—Thomas, served as board member at the M. K. Gandhi Institute

For some, the definition of *well-connected* refers to access to power and wealth. When we prioritize nonviolence at work, being well-connected means having meaningful relationships with our community. It means having authentic interactions with neighbors, and friendship and allyship across diverse groups. It means creative connections with students, artists, media, faith leaders, teachers, local businesses, and many more. Shifting our perspective this way, being well-connected allows us to be part of a bountiful and resilient living system—a teeming web of interactions and ongoing exchanges of knowledge, resources, and support.

In 2012, the Gandhi Institute moved from the University of Rochester campus to a formerly-abandoned house. The house is in a neighborhood that struggles with the impacts of racism, poverty, violence, and gentrification. We hoped the new location would better enable us to achieve our mission to educate, embody, and serve in the broadest possible sense. In many meaningful ways, this has happened.

The location allowed us to support many groups, from serving as a home base for a local 4H group to hosting meetings and workshops for dozens of organizations. Some donate; others use it for free. We offered support and training for area nonprofits, schools, and groups. As a result of seeing ourselves as part of a larger interconnected system and acting that way consistently, our reputation as a community resource grew; neighbors experienced an improved neighborhood climate; donors were more satisfied; staff, volunteers, and board learned and became inspired; and we got to model nonviolence for the greater community.

There was a neighbor that stopped by with her kids for the outdoor community dinner a couple of weeks ago. She had the same sort of reaction to the Institute that I remember having when I first learned about the Institute, what it was about. She received appreciation and acceptance for being there, seeing the garden, the idea of the community dinner as a way to bring people together who might not otherwise cross paths, shared time with one another to talk, and pay attention to one another. There are so many aspects to the Gandhi Institute that are consistently responded to with joy, appreciation, happiness.
—Erin, served as staff at the M. K. Gandhi Institute

When possible, encourage your group or staff (and yourself!) to help others with their projects through fundraising, volunteering, or in other ways. Do this without seeking praise or acknowledgment and see how beautiful and sometimes surprising benefits grow over time.

Your turn: What benefits do you experience in sustaining connections with others? Brainstorm at least three innovative, meaningful ways your group can increase engagement with your communities, both geographic and of practice.

Everything Changes: Impermanence and Living Systems

A year from now the Institute will look different, but I'm not worried about it, even though I like what's here. I feel a sense of comfort and confidence. . . . So many different types of people have come and thrived here. That is something I haven't felt in other places.

—Matt, served as staff at the M. K. Gandhi Institute

In places where we work, worship, and volunteer, there are many ways to embrace the constancy of change. Earlier, we discussed how to hold agreements lightly and allow people to release as needed. Every project, staff member, and endeavor has a life cycle. When upheaval occurs, we have a choice in how we relate to change. The majority of ideas discussed in this book relate to that choice, from knowing our personal operating instructions (especially when stressed) to grief work, from experimentation to soliciting ongoing feedback.

Since the universe is composed of living systems, all things are constantly adapting, evolving, and adjusting to everything else. As we metabolize and act from this understanding, and learn to relax with complexity, possibilities emerge. Our task is to partner with that reality so that, as changes continue to unfold, life on Earth will benefit instead of having to absorb even more harm to this remarkable and—so far as we know—unique planetary home.

This is challenging. It is in our nature to resist change: human brains, emotions, and conditioning prefer stability; they are deep structures that evolved to help us make sense of reality and to navigate it. And yet rigidity in an evolving, interconnected world produces stress and failure, and many scholars note it is increasing in communities and systems.[112] Wherever we spend time, we can help these places grow healthier and more resilient when we learn to relax with change, welcome its potential, and adapt.

---

112. Coleman, *The Way Out: How to Overcome Toxic Polarization*, 60.

Your Turn: What helps you to acknowledge and lower resistance to change? What relationships and practices help you to let go of the comfort of what is familiar?

The Iceberg: Value Shifts and Living Systems

In my gut, I've always known that laws are merely an expression of a society's dominant beliefs. It's the beliefs that we must shift in order for outcomes to change. When policies change in advance of the underlying beliefs, we are often surprised to find the problem still with us.

—Heather McGhee

Only a small portion of an iceberg is visible above the water. It's an apt metaphor for people, and for systems—so much is hidden beneath the surface. Noticing that the bottom of the iceberg is filled with narratives, conscious and unconscious, helps to anchor the understanding that systems live outside *and* within. The bottom of the iceberg also illustrates the presence of the deep structures named earlier.

One colleague who works in schools speaks about this image as a tool in conflict resolution, to help students, staff, and parents see more deeply. Seeing what's under the surface supports people of all ages in recognizing issues, creating community through shared understanding, and searching for solutions to address root causes.

This metaphor can help your organization hold up the mirror to itself too. For example, it helped the Institute in 2016 during a period of painful staff turnover which revealed that, despite a warm interpersonal culture and our collective skill set, our team needed increased structural support to navigate our challenging work and our relationships. As a result, we created the guidelines of our staff commitments and feedback structure. (See page 175.)

As director, I contributed to the problem. I discovered that staff awareness of my busy schedule factored into struggles of some staff to ask for help. I assumed that people would let me know if there were issues, and I was wrong in a couple of significant situations. The affection that some people felt for me also held them back, not wanting to put more on my plate. While looking beneath the waterline of our staff turnover iceberg, I realized that I needed to take a good look at myself. I recognized that I didn't want

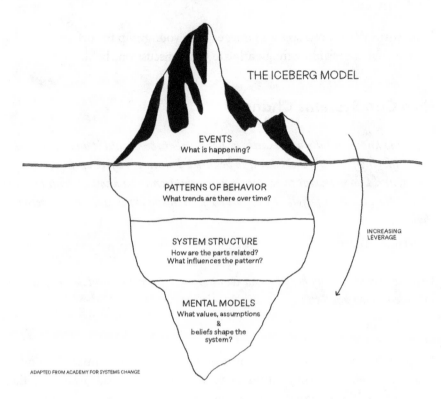

THE ICEBERG MODEL

EVENTS
What is happening?

PATTERNS OF BEHAVIOR
What trends are there over time?

SYSTEM STRUCTURE
How are the parts related?
What influences the pattern?

INCREASING
LEVERAGE

MENTAL MODELS
What values, assumptions
&
beliefs shape the
system?

ADAPTED FROM ACADEMY FOR SYSTEMS CHANGE

to take on more regular meetings with team members and that they were needed. So, in 2019, Erin Thompson, then Chief Operating Officer, stepped into that role for most of the team.

Lack of communication in workplaces and other systems creates a dynamic called a reinforcing loop: communication gets harder, which makes problems worse, which makes it more difficult to communicate. (I'm describing a simple loop. In reality they are more complex.) Making the changes described above, in terms of processes and roles, was an attempt to create a different dynamic: a balancing loop. Actions to increase and respond to information flows—whether internal, interpersonal, or systemic—are examples of balancing loops.[113]

We utilized the iceberg image to unpack reactions to a single event, or to identify consequences and root causes of behavior patterns. The insights generated clarity regarding our values and how to make changes in accordance with them—again working towards finding and shrinking the gap between policy and practice.[114]

113. https://thesystemsthinker.com/reinforcing-and-balancing-loops-building-blocks-of-dynamic-systems/
114. Research demonstrates that connecting change efforts to values supports integration of new ways of knowing, being, and doing: https://doi.org/10.1016/j.jbusvent.2020.106064.

Your Turn: What processes and images help your group to surface and discuss challenges? How frequently are these discussions held?

How Can Systems Change?

I want to know, as fully and exactly as I can, what the wound is and how much I am suffering from it. And I want to be cured; I want to be free of the wound myself, and I do not want to pass it on to my children. . . . I know if I fail to make at least the attempt I forfeit any right to hope that the world will become better than it is now.

—Wendell Berry

God whispered into my heart: if you want to work through nonviolence, you have to proceed with small things, not big.

—M. K. Gandhi

People who are interested in innovation and justice sometimes clash over strategy: whether to work within an existing system, or walk away. Whether you are a healthcare provider struggling with less face time with patients, a reporter trying to deepen your coverage of stories rather than cranking out a required number of words, or a group working on issues of political and social change, this question matters. It's a choice many of us end up making at some point.

I made my choice in 2001 after a week with Dr. Margaret Wheatley. She wrote a book called *Leadership and the New Science*, examining ways that networks (like forest ecosystems, public transit systems, and social change movements) grow, adapt, and maintain themselves. I attended because I had become alarmed that people seem increasingly to serve systems, rather than systems serving people. I asked Dr. Wheatley how systems that no longer optimally serve can be dismantled. Her response was that, by and large, they cannot. In her observation, large systems tend to be resilient and resist change. She suggested that what was most likely to dismantle an existing system was the emergence of a newer, better-performing system. "Life will then vote with its feet," she said.

My next question was: how does one go about creating new systems? The answer she gave is that different networks can become more and more connected, until they become so closely linked that they evolve and form a new, intrinsically networked system. For example, in the Stone Age, small and isolated experiments with metallurgy connected skills through gatherings and trade routes until the primary tools were being made from iron, not stone.

Gandhi understood these dynamics. He coined the phrase "constructive program" and taught it as a framework for change to hundreds of thousands of people during his long career. **Constructive program** is the phrase used to describe nonviolent action taken to build structures, systems, processes, or resources that are positive alternatives to oppression.[115] It can be seen as self-improvement of both community and individual. Constructive program often works alongside obstructive program, which usually involves direct confrontation to, or noncooperation with, oppression. Constructive program is doing what one can to imaginatively and positively create justice within one's own community.

Gandhi helped to organize nineteen constructive programs, including making salt in defiance of the British monopoly on salt production and handspinning cotton while refusing to buy imported British cloth. Another example of a constructive program is how Cesar Chavez, Dolores Huerta, and the United Farmworkers formed a credit union to help farm workers get small loans. At the Institute, we built a community garden in the middle of a neighborhood defined as a food desert, offering free organic vegetables.

Echoing Wheatley's admonition on building the new system, Gandhi said that protest campaigns without constructive programs will be "like a paralyzed hand attempting to lift a spoon."[116] He recommended the 80/20 rule—spend 80 percent of your energy building the new system through constructive programs, and 20 percent on opposing injustice with nonviolent action. Many restorative justice practitioners recommend the same as ideal: 80 percent of effort on building relationships and caring for community, 20 percent on response to conflicts. Restorative work in classrooms, schools, and organizations is another example of constructive programs.

This framework of Gandhi's and that brief conversation with Dr. Wheatley helped me to embrace a focus of both/and rather than either/or. At BayNVC in Oakland and later at the Gandhi Institute in Rochester,

115. https://archives.mettacenter.org/definitions/constructive-program/
116. M. K. Gandhi, "Constructive Programme: Its Meaning and Place," https://www.jmu.edu/gandhi-center/wm_library/gandhiana-constprog.pdf.

my colleagues and I were privileged to work on building new systems, experimenting all the way. At the same time we worked with thousands of individuals choosing to make changes from within. In both contexts, the idea of nurturing the work of those around me, not just my own, became a central focus. I saw that helping those "discrete networks" connect to amplify their work was critically important. This understanding became a core principle in organizing resources at the Gandhi Institute and of putting nonviolence to work.

Your Turn: Do you notice examples of this 80/20 principle in any of the work you care about? How can you use your resources of time, experience, and influence to help others' efforts, without seeking credit?

Chapter Nine Key Ideas

- Learning to see and appreciate living systems helps us make far better choices.
- Rather than trying to simplify situations, learn to relax with complexity.
- Permaculture principles, like stacking function, encourage whole-systems thinking.
- Edge effect is another permaculture principle that encourages us to foster and respect the high degree of diversity that naturally occurs where differences meet.
- Feedback, especially through the use of structured processes, reminds everyone that they matter and their choices count. It also counters conflict aversion that most of us struggle with.
- Many of us need to unlearn tendencies toward competition to make room for wholehearted collaboration.
- Helping others fosters relationships and connections that grow over time.
- Though humans resist change, adapting and welcoming its potential fosters resilience.
- The Iceberg Model is a generative, participatory way to dig into how systems work.
- Find your own balance between addressing existing problems and building new systems.

Conclusion

The staff are living and practicing nonviolence in their lives which is a very good thing. That's how we're going to teach people: through living it, not just speaking about it. It's a long road because nonviolence, as Grandfather said, is still so new and people don't know the depths of it. So every day you wake up and find something new in the philosophy, which is what he found.

—Arun Gandhi, cofounder of the M. K. Gandhi Institute

We're running out of time. Even as we speak, the circle of violence is closing in. Either way, change will come. It could be bloody, or it could be beautiful. It depends on us.

—Arundhati Roy

In her wonderful, essential book *Hospicing Modernity*, author Vanessa Machado de Oliveira contrasts mastery and depth education. She defines mastery education as akin to filling a cup, and depth education as "a mode of engagement designed to prompt us to dig deeper and to relate wider."[117] I hope you have experienced both types of learning in these pages.

If you don't see yourself *yet* as having the influence to change a group's or organization's functioning, practice with the "inside job" and value shifts perspectives, and see what happens for your well-being and for your ability to positively influence others. Be courageous and invite people to experiment. Most of us underestimate the power we have, and won't know until we try. Adapt for the conditions you operate within. Most of all, hang onto this vision: groups and workplaces can support wholeness, meaning, learning, and healing. They can generate positive change in human society.

117. Vanessa Machado de Oliveira, *Hospicing Modernity: Facing Humanity's Wrongs and the Implications for Social Activism*, 44.

My relationship, communication-wise, in the last five years (we've been together fifteen) has been transformed. We're much healthier in how we talk to each other, how we fight. The Institute changed that for me.

—Alex, served as staff at the M. K. Gandhi Institute

As Alex notes, this way of working offers substantial benefits. Their statement helped fuel my interest in writing this book. As I get clearer about these principles and live from them, it reduces the drag of uncertainty, shame, and self-judgment from my social conditioning and painful early experiences. Years of interactions with colleagues, hundreds of talks and workshops, the interviews for this project, and a growing body of research in numerous fields boost my confidence that they can help us during these dynamic and difficult times.

I can't wait to hear whether these notes were helpful to you—please share your thoughts! If you want to try a feedback process we use at the Institute, send your pluses (what worked), your deltas (what would have increased learning/engagement), and your bright ideas to kit@gandhiinstitute.org.

I have come to think of Mohandas Gandhi and of Dr. Martin Luther King Jr. as prophets who foretold the consequences of unchecked violence in human culture. I reflect on Dr. King's words in a 1967 speech, calling on each of us to be "creatively maladjusted" to violence and discrimination. I write these words as the world watches the destruction of Gaza and the destruction of countless relationships as the division over the questions of justice and safety continue. Within these pages are ideas and practices that can help us move toward a world that works for all. I sincerely hope at least one idea supports you, over time, to become creatively maladjusted, for the good of all life, and to keep faith with the unknowable future.

This comes with love,
Kit

Appendix 1

Project Stories: Proof of Concept Experiments

Conflict resolution in the Gandhian sense does not come about primarily through confrontation of views, dialogue, bargaining, and compromise, but through experimentation with new forms of social life.

—Johan Galtung

The Power of Near-Peer Education

Principles: experimentation, trust, collaboration

People teaching each other: young people teaching college students teaching high school, high school teaching middle school—everyone was a teacher.

—Skylar, served as staff at the M. K. Gandhi Institute

In early 2010, we clarified that one of our organization's primary areas of focus was to teach people ages 12–24 the principles and practices of nonviolence. An opportunity that we began to recognize, which later became an important principle of our work, was the power of "near-peer" educators. We saw how middle school students responded to learning from high school students, how high school students responded to college students, and how college students especially enjoyed learning from young adults in their twenties. This insight led to several important outcomes over time.

1. We skewed the hiring of Gandhi staff toward younger educators overall, seeing that both younger audiences and adults would benefit from being led and taught by younger leaders.
2. From 2010 to 2018, we supported a "Gandhi Service Fellowship" for high school and college students in the local area who wanted an immersive,

ten-month study. Ultimately, over forty young leaders received intensive mentoring, learning, and opportunities to apply their knowledge.

3. We created a project called the Summer Youth Facilitators' Institute (SYFI) from 2016–2018, employing 3–5 youth to learn and teach children, other youth, and adults. We prioritized hiring youth from Rochester schools who received formal and on-the-job training in facilitation and nonviolence, and who participated in service learning in the Gandhi gardens, as well as numerous creative projects.

4. We built partnerships with the local Americorps programs and other youth organizations, offering free and low-cost training for their staff to leverage their collective influence in working with thousands of youth in the area.

Some programs phased out over time. This felt right to us as new projects and priorities emerged for staff, and as we shifted to better meet the needs of the community as we perceived them.

Gandhi and Nonviolence Cards

Principles: local economy, experiential education, respecting funds of knowledge

Experiential education was the best approach to connect with younger people, and also worked wonderfully with older adults. We began to hunt for experiential ways for young people and adults to learn more about Gandhi. In 2011, we found a deck of cards that was used to teach about the US civil rights movement and decided to create a similar deck about Gandhi's life, values, and efforts.

One of my colleagues wrote the copy and another made images from a collection of old black and white photos of Gandhi and the Self-Rule Movement that had been donated to the Institute years before. An amazing volunteer, talented graphic designer Bob Kiesow, donated his gifts to design the packaging and the cards themselves. Drawing upon the insights about learning and brain functioning in Daniel Kahnemann's book *Thinking Fast and Slow*, we reduced the use of Sanskrit and Hindi phrases and made the language plain and user-friendly for middle school audiences. We did this by testing the wording with a few people in that age group, and by running it by teachers. Each card featured a quote, a short educational passage, and a reflection question.

Rather than trying to print the cards as cheaply as possible, we employed a printer in Rochester to print the cards and packaging. Even though we operated on a very tight budget, this choice aligned with our value of supporting the local economy.

In the years since, the Gandhi Cards have traveled the world and accompanied me on one of my two visits speaking at the United Nations on Gandhi's birthday. They have been translated into three languages so far and there is an online version as well.

The popularity of these cards declined with the increase in "call out" culture, which included Gandhi's racist language regarding Black South Africans in his first years in that country. Gandhi was quick to call himself out in his autobiography, and asked when he died that all of his books and other writings be burned. He did not want to be a saint and, increasingly, his wish has been granted.

Youth Healing Hate Grants

Principles: recognizing/undermining adultism, trust, collaboration, support

This project grew out of a question at the conclusion of workshops called "Let's Talk About Hate," inspired by reading Howard Thurman's book *Jesus and the Disinherited*. This is a book that Dr. King is said to have carried with him during the last years of his life. One chapter focuses primarily on hatred, and includes the sentence, "There is a danger to any society when hatred has become respectable." After reading that sentence, I felt a call to action. We held reading groups using this book and then created the "Let's Talk About Hate" offering.

To move the conversation to action, our final exercise in that workshop was to ask participants to design a project with the assumption that each of them could receive $5000 to reduce hate. So many wonderful ideas emerged that in 2017 we created the Youth Healing Hate grants of $1000 for Monroe County youth aged 12–24.

During the first year, we received several applications that included funding for necessary tech in their budget. Seeing this, a supporter asked whether we could know if youth were applying just to get new, high-value items, or if the tech should be returned at the end of the project to prevent them from taking advantage of the grant. These concerns highlighted how uncommon it was to trust youth to be financially responsible and to see their projects through. Though the grants had the potential to empower youth, we had to challenge unconscious adultism, racism, and classism to make sure our impact matched our intent.

As of February 2024, thirty-nine projects have been funded. Check out the specific projects at the Gandhi Institute website. I am delighted that Pace e Bene created a similar program in 2022, with great success.[118]

Nonviolence Now Media Project

Principles: generosity, humility, collaboration, social change via positive news

The Institute is giving people a glimpse of what they don't even know they are missing.
—Joel, served as board member at the M. K. Gandhi Institute

In December 2017, the Gandhi Institute unexpectedly won a national contest sponsored by the Newman's Own Foundation. Despite being one of the smallest organizations of the hundreds that participated, we received third prize, in part due to the efforts of Jamie Rudd who came to us as part of Americorps VISTA, then joined staff. The prize was $250,000 in global digital banner ads.

Rather than promoting the Gandhi Institute through this windfall, we decided to use the prize to promote the idea of nonviolence especially to younger audiences. Furthermore, given that the campaign was international, we wanted to recognize and take responsibility for the United States' global contribution to violence. Accordingly, we featured other organizations' work on the website and other materials that backed up the ads.

The collective response to this approach of generosity and humility led to beautiful outcomes that continue to strengthen my faith in humanity and my willingness to stand for collaboration. Here's what happened:

---

118. https://paceebene.org/changemaker-grants

1. The media company coordinating the prizes decided to double the donation. They were inspired by our use of the gift, to highlight non-violence principles in lieu of advancing our organization. That company also donated a full page ad on the inside front cover of Newsweek magazine in December 2018.
2. We were invited by the Indian embassy to formally initiate the media campaign on Gandhi's 149th birthday (October 2, 2018) at the United Nations.
3. Amazing project volunteer Rivera Sun, who was compiling stories of global nonviolence to share via the project's social media channels, found so many underreported stories that she launched a sister project called Nonviolence News in 2019.
4. We received an additional grant to support a nationwide digital ad campaign focused on the top twenty-five cities in the United States that were most impacted by violence in 2019. The call-to-action in the digital ads was to support the Peace Alliance Blueprint for Peace effort, and to increase the readership of Nonviolence News. This campaign increased readership to over 90,000 subscribers.
5. In March 2020, at the onset of the pandemic, we brought the Non-violence Now campaign to our local community of Rochester, New York. In collaboration with several partners, including the city and county governments, we put up a series of billboard and public bus ads calling upon residents to be their best selves. This Nonviolence Now campaign strategically invoked the concept of being more nonviolent without explicitly saying the word, using related phrases like "keep your cool." The campaign repeated in 2021 with the addition of lawn signs as well as buses and billboards.
6. In 2022, we nominated Nonviolence News for an international journalism awards program, Pioneers In United Nations Sustainable Development Goals. It won first place out of the eighty-five projects nominated from sixty-one countries, received a $2,000 award to support its work, and showcased Nonviolence Now and Nonviolence News to 14,000+ people around the world.

Bright Spots Inventory

Principles: collaboration; inclusion; state the dream, not the nightmare; social change via positive news

Since 2010, Gandhi Institute staff have worked with a host of community partners and educators in Rochester city schools to address school climate and to create cultures of peace within schools. Among the most inspiring projects were Positive Assets (aka Bright Spots) Inventories. These were daylong, intensive, appreciative inquiry efforts within a single school building to examine school climate. They began in 2017 and continued through 2019.

In collaboration with Eagle Rock School located in Estes Park, Colorado, and RCSD's Roc Restorative Team, Institute staff conducted several Positive Assets Inventories. Eagle Rock is a national hub for educational reform and best practices who provide pro bono training and mentoring.

In three-hour sessions, a trained team conducted student and teacher focus groups and gathered hundreds of low inference observations about positive relationships and the use of restorative practices in the school. In the afternoon, the team input their data and compiled a draft report of findings. This was presented to the school principal and other key personnel within a week of the session, providing swift, positive feedback.

This project boosted efforts to change school climate in three ways:

1. Committed, often heroic efforts by teachers and administrators are frequently unacknowledged. These inventories helped to correct that imbalance.
2. Most data gathered in relation to school climate efforts is quantitative, or numbers based. This project provided a detailed, fresh, "on the ground" qualitative look at what was going on inside schools. This was useful in helping to inform change and improvement efforts.
3. Globally, experts in social innovation, such as the Skoll Centre for Social Entrepreneurship at Oxford, recommend change efforts that leverage existing bright spots in low-performing systems. The inventories we conducted applied the best practices of a global field to our local community.

We partnered with Ruth Turner, then Chief of Student Support Services in the Rochester City School District, and her staff to conduct these inventories, along with staff and youth organizers from a community partner called Teen Empowerment. Gandhi Institute staff became well-versed in the preparation, data gathering techniques, and reporting necessary to implement this project. Because this is low-cost, participatory research, it offers opportunities for a variety of individuals to participate and to see schools firsthand.

Appendix 2
Gandhi Staff Commitments and Feedback Form

Staff Commitments June 2020

1. We practice cultural humility by realizing that we are never done learning about what it means for ourselves and others to live in a society of systemic, interpersonal, and internalized oppression. This comes from our recognition that the Gandhi Institute currently exists within a white supremacist, heterosexist, patriarchal, etc. society.
2. We strive to bring our whole selves to meetings; we share authentically about how we feel, without needing to give all the details. We recognize that unexpressed emotions can easily be misinterpreted.
3. When tensions and challenges arise between us, we work to quickly acknowledge and address them with the other person. We ask for support if needed because we recognize that persistent challenges between individuals may represent larger organizational issues. Thus, requesting support for challenges benefits everyone.
4. We encourage one another to offer supportive positive and critical feedback regarding current and/or proposed projects, ideas, and strategies. These feedback-giving processes typically begin at staff meetings, and other meetings; however, we encourage one another to offer feedback in any context when it can be given with care and respect.

Conflict Process (proposed)

- When any person on staff begins to struggle in some way with another team member, they are requested to get some support and talk to that person as soon as possible. (Walk toward conflicts when they are small.)
- If after a conversation the issue is not resolved in a good way, these two agree to ask a mutually agreeable third person to help them connect.

(This person does not have to be a Gandhi Institute staff member—board members/friends of the Institute have also served in this role.)

- If after a good faith effort has been made the underlying challenge/concerns remain, the issue is now considered to be an issue for the team as a whole (see item 3 above) and we hold a restorative process with as many people as make sense to participate.

M. K. Gandhi Institute Feedback Form

Find a downloadable version of this form at paceebene.org/culture-shift.

SECTIONS	ACTIONS/EXPERIENCES	NEEDS MET/UNMET
INTRAPERSONAL		
O Timeliness O Preparedness O Personal Calendar O Authentic Presence O Skills Growth O Initiative O Self-Care		
INTERPERSONAL		
O Willingness to hear impact on others O Vulnerability O Multiformat Communication O Organization O Time Management O Boundaries O Tidiness O Facilitation Skills O Active Listening O Body Language O Nonviolent Communication Use O Team Work O Leadership O Take/Make Space O Walking Towards Conflict (During/After)		
INSTITUTIONAL		
O Inclusion of all voices O Awareness to group dynamic O Team Work O Learning Time O Chores O Group Engagement O Nonviolence Education O Restorative Practices O Environmental Sustainability O Modeling Cultural Humility, re:own Rank/Privilege O Integrating Anti-Racist/ Anti-Oppressive structures into programming O Examining & restructuring practices and systems for inclusivity within Institute & beyond O Participating in community/ structural initiatives equity&justice re: race, gender, sexual identity, class, etc.		

Resources

Books

Coleman, Peter T. *The Way Out: How to Overcome Toxic Polarization.* Columbia University Press, 2021.

Easwaran, Eknath. *A Man to Match His Mountains: Badshah Khan, Nonviolent Soldier of Islam.* Nilgiri Press, 1985.

Easwaran, Eknath. *Gandhi the Man: The Story of His Transformation.* Nilgiri Press, 1997.

Fosl, Catherine. *Subversive Southerner: Anne Braden and the Struggle for Racial Justice in the Cold War South.* University Press of Kentucky, 2006.

Gandhi, Arun. *The Gift of Anger: And Other Lessons from My Grandfather Mahatma Gandhi.* Gallery/Jeter Publishing 2017.

Gandhi, Mohandas K. *Gandhi: An Autobiography—The Story of My Experiments With Truth.* Beacon Press, 1993.

Haga, Kazu. *Healing Resistance: A Radically Different Response to Harm.* Parallax Press, 2020.

Horton, Myles and Paulo Freire. *We Make the Road by Walking: Conversations on Education and Social Change.* Temple University Press, 1990.

Horton, Myles with Judith Kohl and Herbert Kohl. *The Long Haul: An Autobiography.* Teachers College Press, 1997.

King Jr., Dr. Martin Luther. *Where Do We Go From Here: Chaos or Community?* Beacon Press, 2010.

Machada de Oliveira, Vanessa. *Hospicing Modernity: Facing Humanity's Wrongs and the Implications for Social Activism.* North Atlantic Books, 2021.

Macy, Joanna. *World as Lover, World as Self: Courage for Global Justice and Ecological Renewal.* Parallax Press, 2007.

Mandela, Nelson. *Long Walk to Freedom: The Autobiography of Nelson Mandela.* Back Bay Books, 1995.

Manning, Roxy and Sarah Peyton. *The Antiracist Heart: A Self-Compassion and Activism Handbook.* Berrett-Koehler Publishers, 2023.

Menakem, Resmaa. *My Grandmother's Hands: Racialized Trauma and the Pathway to Mending Our Hearts and Bodies*. Central Recovery Press, 2017.

Mindell, Arnold. *Sitting in the Fire: Large Group Transformation Using Conflict and Diversity*. Deep Democracy Exchange, 2014.

Mitchell, Sherri. *Sacred Instructions: Indigenous Wisdom for Living Spirit-Based Change*. North Atlantic Books, 2018.

Mohawk, John. *Thinking in Indian: A John Mohawk Reader*. Fulcrum Publishing, 2010.

Nagler, Michael. *The Search for a Nonviolent Future: A Promise of Peace for Ourselves, Our Families, and Our World*. New World Library, 2004.

Olton, Gwendolyn. *From Conflict to Community: Transforming Conflicts Without Authorities*. Microcosm Publishing, 2022.

Perry, Bruce D. and Oprah Winfrey. *What Happened to You?: Conversations on Trauma, Resilience, and Healing*. Flatiron Books: An Oprah Book, 2021.

Ripley, Amanda. *High Conflict: Why We Get Trapped and How We Get Out*. Simon and Schuster, 2021.

Rosenberg, Marshall. *Nonviolent Communication: A Language of Compassion*. Puddledancer Press, 1999.

Somé, Malidoma Patrice. *Rituals: Power, Healing and Community*. Penguin Books, 1997.

Stroh, David Peter. *Systems Thinking For Social Change: A Practical Guide to Solving Complex Problems, Avoiding Unintended Consequences, and Achieving Lasting Results*. Chelsea Green Publishing, 2015.

Suarez, Cyndi. *The Power Manual: How to Master Complex Power Dynamics*. New Society Publishers, 2018.

Thurman, Howard. *Jesus and the Disinherited*. Beacon Press, 1996.

Weller, Francis and Michael Lerner. *The Wild Edge of Sorrow: Rituals of Renewal and the Sacred Work of Grief*. North Atlantic Books, 2015.

Yunkaporta, Tyson. *Sand Talk: How Indigenous Thinking Can Save the World*. Harper Collins, 2021.

Online

Barefoot College, https://www.barefootcollege.org/
Bureau of Linguistical Reality, https://bureauoflinguisticalreality.com/
Erica Chenoweth, https://www.ericachenoweth.com/
M. K. Gandhi Institute, https://gandhiinstitute.org/
Nonviolence News, https://nonviolencenews.org/

About Pace e Bene and Campaign Nonviolence

Pace e Bene Nonviolence Service's mission is to foster justice, peace, and the well-being of all through education, resources, and action for nonviolent change.

Founded in 1989 by the Franciscan Friars of California, Pace e Bene Nonviolence Service is now an independent, non-denominational, nonprofit organization spreading the power of nonviolence.

"Pace e Bene" (pronounced "pah-chay bay-nay") is an Italian greeting from St. Francis and St. Clare of Assisi meaning "Peace and all Good." It is a blessing, a hope, and a way of acknowledging the sacredness of those whom we encounter.

For decades Pace e Bene has led trainings around the world, created resources for change, and organized many campaigns and movements for nonviolence.

In 2014 Pace e Bene launched its most comprehensive project yet—Campaign Nonviolence, a long-term movement for a culture of active nonviolence, connecting the dots between war, poverty, racism, and environmental destruction.

Through Campaign Nonviolence, we organize The Nonviolent Cities Project and the annual Campaign Nonviolence Action Days, where every September we mobilize across the country and around the world for a culture of peace, economic equality, racial justice, and environmental healing.

Help build Campaign Nonviolence by studying nonviolence, including Pace e Bene's books; inviting Pace e Bene speakers to your community; taking trainings and organizing events; supporting this work financially; and taking nonviolent action for a new culture of nonviolence.

For further information, visit paceebene.org, email: info@paceebene.org, call: 510-268-8765.

Other titles by Pace e Bene Press

Engaging Nonviolence: Activating Nonviolent Change in Our Lives and Our World

Radical Prayers: On Peace, Love, and Nonviolence

Nonviolent Lives: People and Movements Changing the World Through the Power of Active Nonviolence

The Nonviolent Life

Love is What Matters: Writings on Peace and Nonviolence

Engage: Exploring Nonviolent Living

From Violence to Wholeness

Traveling with the Turtle: Women's Spirituality and Peacemaking

Living with the Wolf: Walking the Way of Nonviolence

Franciscan Nonviolence: Stories, Reflections, Principles, Practices, and Resources

About the Author

Kit Miller is director emeritus of the M. K. Gandhi Institute for Nonviolence, after having served as executive director 2009–2021. The work and reach of the Institute expanded greatly under her stewardship. Prior to the Institute, she worked as director/celebrator of Bay Area Nonviolent Communication in Oakland, California. Currently, Kit serves as a facilitator and educator for a variety of organizations, mainly in education, healthcare, and NGOs. Much of that time is dedicated to conflict work within teams.

9 780997 833737